Simply Chinggis

Simply Chinggis

TIMOTHY MAY

SIMPLY CHARLY
NEW YORK

Copyright © 2021 by Timothy May

Cover Illustration by José Ramos
Cover Design by Scarlett Rugers

All rights reserved. No part of this publication may be reproduced, distributed, or transmitted in any form or by any means, including photocopying, recording, or other electronic or mechanical methods, without the prior written permission of the publisher, except in the case of brief quotations embodied in critical reviews and certain other noncommercial uses permitted by copyright law. For permission requests, write to the publisher at the address below.

permissions@simplycharly.com

ISBN: 978-1-943657-62-9

Brought to you by http://simplycharly.com

Contents

Praise for *Simply Chinggis*	vii
Other *Great Lives*	ix
Series Editor's Foreword	x
Preface	xi

1.	Chinggis Khan as Child (1162-1182)	1
2.	Chinggis Khan as Temüjin (1182–1187)	15
3.	The Rise of Chinggis Khan (1196-1206)	26
4.	Creation of the Yeke Monggol Ulus	42
5.	Campaigns of Chinggis Khan (1205-1227)	52
6.	Family Matters	76
7.	The Art of War	98
8.	The Wit and Wisdom of Chinggis Khan	107
9.	Chinggis vs. Genghis	116
10.	Legacy of Chinggis Khan	123

Sources	133
Suggested Reading	137
About the Author	146
A Word from the Publisher	147

Praise for *Simply Chinggis*

"Timothy May provides the reader with an accessible introduction to one of history's most renowned figures. He offers a balanced portrait of Chinggis Khan, describing both the destruction the conqueror wrought, as well as his contributions to global history. May writes with readable prose and supplies apt and colorful references to modern people and events."

—**Morris Rossabi, author of *Khubilai Khan: His Life and Times***

"In this book written for a popular audience, Timothy May, a recognized expert on the Mongols, does much more than chronicle the well-known facts about the great conqueror. He brings vividly to life the world in which Chinggis Khan was born and rose to power. Unlike earlier biographers, he gives a full analysis of the family dynamics, which helped to shape Mongol rule for centuries. This is an excellent introduction to the world of the steppe and the life of one of the world's greatest conquerors."

—**Beatrice Manz, Professor of History, Tufts University**

"Chinggis ("Ocean") Khan not only created by sheer force of personality the largest contiguous land empire in history, but also at the same time laid down foundations for the intensive exchanges of things and ideas that were to follow. In so doing, he became very much the founder of our modern global age. Without him, history would have been very different. Tim May has now not only produced the best biography to date, but also provides much more than a simple biography, making his book an introduction to the other sides of what made Chinggis Khan Chinggis Khan."

—**Paul Buell, author of *The A to Z of the Mongol World Empire* and *Historical Dictionary of the Mongolian World Empire***

"There are few people who can claim to have had a greater impact on world history than Chinggis Khan, which makes sketching his biography simultaneously very desirable and daunting for scholars. *Simply Chinggis* renders this complex topic into an easily understandable and highly engaging introduction to the Mongol ruler's life and achievements. This witty and thought-provoking work is imminently readable, as Timothy May's keen eye for detail and colorful descriptions help to reconstruct some of the major events in the Mongol khan's military and political career, whilst also providing insights into his decision-making and strategy. Throughout the book, May sacrifices nothing in the way of rigorous analysis or historical methodology. Rather, '*Simply Chinggis*' sees one of the foremost scholars of the early Mongol Empire at the top of his game, drawing on an extensive list of primary sources and the latest research to tackle some of the most perplexing aspects of Chinggis Khan's life. Readers of this biography will be rewarded with a rich insight into the story behind one of the world's foremost political and military leaders."

—**Michael Hope, Associate Professor of Asian History, Yonsei University, Underwood International College**

"Timothy May proves an able guide through the complex politics and events of Chinggis Khan's rise to power; and to the key personalities, issues and interpretations, providing contextual knowledge aimed to enhance the reader's understanding both of what was happening and why it happened."

—**Angus Stewart, Lecturer in Middle Eastern History, University of St Andrews**

Other *Great Lives*

Simply Austen by Joan Klingel Ray
Simply Beckett by Katherine Weiss
Simply Beethoven by Leon Plantinga
Simply Chekhov by Carol Apollonio
Simply Chomsky by Raphael Salkie
Simply Chopin by William Smialek
Simply Darwin by Michael Ruse
Simply Descartes by Kurt Smith
Simply Dickens by Paul Schlicke
Simply Dirac by Helge Kragh
Simply Eliot by Joseph Maddrey
Simply Euler by Robert E. Bradley
Simply Faulkner by Philip Weinstein
Simply Fitzgerald by Kim Moreland
Simply Freud by Stephen Frosh
Simply Gödel by Richard Tieszen
Simply Hegel by Robert L. Wicks
Simply Hitchcock by David Sterritt
Simply Joyce by Margot Norris
Simply Machiavelli by Robert Fredona
Simply Napoleon by J. David Markham & Matthew Zarzeczny
Simply Nietzsche by Peter Kail
Simply Proust by Jack Jordan
Simply Riemann by Jeremy Gray
Simply Sartre by David Detmer
Simply Tolstoy by Donna Tussing Orwin
Simply Stravinsky by Pieter van den Toorn
Simply Turing by Michael Olinick
Simply Wagner by Thomas S. Grey
Simply Wittgenstein by James C. Klagge

Series Editor's Foreword

Simply Charly's "Great Lives" series offers brief but authoritative introductions to the world's most influential people—scientists, artists, writers, economists, and other historical figures whose contributions have had a meaningful and enduring impact on our society.

Each book provides an illuminating look at the works, ideas, personal lives, and the legacies these individuals left behind, also shedding light on the thought processes, specific events, and experiences that led these remarkable people to their groundbreaking discoveries or other achievements. Additionally, every volume explores various challenges they had to face and overcome to make history in their respective fields, as well as the little-known character traits, quirks, strengths, and frailties, myths, and controversies that sometimes surrounded these personalities.

Our authors are prominent scholars and other top experts who have dedicated their careers to exploring each facet of their subjects' work and personal lives.

Unlike many other works that are merely descriptions of the major milestones in a person's life, the "Great Lives" series goes above and beyond the standard format and content. It brings substance, depth, and clarity to the sometimes complex lives and works of history's most powerful and influential people.

We hope that by exploring this series, readers will not only gain new knowledge and understanding of what drove these geniuses, but also find inspiration for their own lives. Isn't this what a great book is supposed to do?

Charles Carlini, Simply Charly
New York City

Preface

Simply Chinggis. A rather odd title that could be a slogan for a vodka advertising campaign. And yes, Chinggis Khan does indeed have his own vodka brand. On the surface, it seems an unlikely title for a book about the Mongolian conqueror. Why not *Simply Chinggis Khan*? Or *Simply Temüjin*? After all, in the Mongolian language of the day, Chinggis Khan means "firm or fierce lord," or perhaps "oceanic lord," but the man who used that particular sobriquet was known throughout his childhood and early adulthood as Temüjin. For one thing, no one would buy a book called *Simply Temüjin*, except perhaps out of idle curiosity to find out who this person was—particularly if the book's cover lives up to the standards of the others in this series. Indeed, the only people who know Temüjin in casual conversation would be those who have read a book on Chinggis Khan.

So why not *Simply Genghis Khan*, as the Mongolian conqueror is commonly known? For starters, it is not his name nor his title. It is a corruption of Chinggis Khan. Additionally, this author is adamantly against using the G-word and has taught legions of students to castigate those who use it. Furthermore, as my son was gently reprimanded when correcting his world history teacher after the latter referred to Chinggis as Genghis, I should hold up my end of the bargain and not blaspheme. There are other valid reasons as well, which should please the publisher of this book, who raised his own valid concerns about not using the dreaded G-word; I will divulge these reasons in a later chapter. Until then, I shall trust that the reader will make the adjustment while reading in anticipation of this "revelation."

More importantly, this book is about one of the most influential figures in world history, at least in the last millennium, and as such, he deserves every respect and consideration. Indeed, he was fierce not only in the traditional sense—cruel and bloodthirsty—but also "fierce" as defined in *The Urban Dictionary*, bold in his actions. Thus, *Simply Chinggis* is more than an adequate title for the life of Chinggis Khan.

If one takes a casual perusal of Chinggis Khan's early life, there is nothing to suggest that he would become one of the truly pivotal figures in world history. His life (c.1158–1227) was full of drama: they murdered his father when Temüjin was only 8 or 9 years old; his family was largely ostracized; young Temüjin killed his elder stepbrother and was enslaved as a result but eventually escaped; they stole his wife from him and he did not regain her for several months. Although he rose to power, he lost it after one battle against his former best friend. At that point, he should have disappeared from history ... and in fact, he did disappear for 10 years. We only have hints of where he was at the time, but we do not know what he did or with whom he associated. Yet, when Temüjin returned, he proved to be not only more mature, but also more determined as well. One might even say "fiercer." No longer was he the pawn of others, but a man who made his own destiny.

The wars that followed in Mongolia unified the steppes under his rule. Although it is not apparent that Chinggis Khan planned to conquer the world, his armies conquered more territory than any other commander in world history. His children and grandchildren expanded the empire even more so that it spanned from Korea to Bulgaria, from the Persian Gulf and the South China Sea to the Siberian tundra, establishing an empire of approximately the size of Africa—almost 12 million square miles. Yet, Chinggis Khan was more than a mere conqueror, for he founded a state.

While the Mongol Empire lasted in some permutation for over 150 years, the notion of Mongolia endured. Before Chinggis Khan, the territory that is present-day Mongolia was simply the pastures of various nomadic groups. Empires rose and fell, and the identities of the groups dwelling there changed with time. Yet, after Chinggis Khan, only Mongols remained. Indeed, without him, there would be no Mongols. His legacy even survived 70 years of communist rule in the 20th century. To this day, he has remained very much present in the minds of Mongolians, who consider him as their founding father. While he did not do it alone, he was the genius of the State.

The rest of the world has mixed feelings about Chinggis Khan and the Mongol Empire in general. Prior to the late 20th century, the common view, especially among those living in the territory of the former Mongol Empire, was that Chinggis Khan was a destructive force; after all, he famously said, "I am the punishment of God ... If you had not committed great sins, God would not have sent a punishment like me upon you."

A more balanced reading of the sources, however, reveals that Chinggis Khan, like all people, was a much more complex figure. While the destruction he wrought can never be ignored, he was so much more than merely a villain: he was also a statesman, a visionary, a hero, a husband, father, and leader who sought to create a stable Mongolia and protect it from the machinations of outside forces that had contributed so much to the turmoil that had shaped his early life. Thus, this book not only examines his life, but also considers how the events and people Chinggis Khan encountered molded and influenced the decisions he made, which, in turn, changed the course of history.

Chinggis Khan first entered my life in fifth grade, when I stumbled upon the old Harold Lamb children's biography of the great Mongol leader titled *Genghis Khan and the Mongol Horde* (1954). While Lamb's biography is now outdated (as it was in my childhood), he wrote with such enthusiasm that one could not help but be captivated. While Chinggis Khan lingered in my memory for years, it was not until my senior year at the College of William & Mary that I immersed myself in the study of Chinggis Khan and the Mongol Empire. And the rest, as they say, is history. I can only hope that this book might have a similar effect on others as well.

Timothy May
Dahlonega, GA

1. Chinggis Khan as Child (1162-1182)

On August 18, 1227, Chinggis Khan lay sweating from a fever in his bed in the kingdom of Xi Xia, which he invaded and conquered 18 years earlier.

Now almost 65 years old and ill, the emperor may have wished to be closer to home, in the cooler climate of northern Mongolia. There, one of his grandchildren or wives could have cooled his brow with a cloth soaked in the water from the Onan-Kerulen River Basin, where Chinggis Khan was born and which served as the cradle of the Mongol Empire that existed only due to the efforts of the man wracked with fever, dying far from home.

Xi Xia is on the frontiers of Mongolia in what are now Ningxia and Gansu provinces in the People's Republic of China. Fourteen years after Mongol armies vanquished Xi Xia, a kingdom ruled by the Tangut, a people of Tibetan origin, its rulers rebelled when Chinggis Khan's viceroy died and while Chinggis Khan was far away in Central Asia.

Chinggis Khan attempted to resolve the matter diplomatically, but negotiations failed. He realized Xi Xia would never fully accept Mongol rule as long as its own royal family existed, although the Mongols had not occupied the region in 1209 but rather agreed to accept tribute. With no other recourse but war, the Mongols invaded in 1226. Neither army nor fortresses could halt the Mongol advance, but the Tangut escaped total destruction. Taking a break from the campaign, the now elderly Chinggis Khan went hunting. When some *qulan*—wild asses—suddenly emerged from the brush, his startled horse reared and flung the Mongol leader. The fall did not kill him, but he suffered internal injuries. Although his generals and sons attempted to persuade him to cease the campaign, he refused, telling them not to stop until Xi Xia had been "maimed and tamed," even if he died. The question was, which would expire first, Chinggis Khan or Xi Xia?

In the meantime, his generals, family, and perhaps even he himself, reflected on how Chinggis Khan, a boy from an obscure tribe in a remote Mongol region conquered the largest territory in history, dwarfing the exploits of Cyrus the Great, Alexander the Great, and Napoleon Bonaparte. He created the largest connected empire in history, exceeded only in total landmass by the British Empire, which was not contiguous. Conquest and military force alone are not enough to build empires; this task also requires genius. Chinggis Khan had plenty of that, but his brilliance would have been wasted if he had not learned valuable lessons from his life's experiences.

History reveals that Chinggis Khan's childhood was difficult, and it undoubtedly shaped many of his beliefs and core values. Then again, who doesn't experience hardships? How we respond to them often becomes a defining character trait. In many ways, Chinggis Khan's life was one of rags-to-riches on an unimaginable scale. He had what some might consider a dysfunctional childhood—before the age of 15, he lived through the murder of his father, ostracism and abandonment, poverty, fratricide, captivity, enslavement, and robbery. If Chinggis Khan had not risen to these challenges, you would not be reading this book—any of these experiences could have erased Temüjin from history. Yet persevere he did.

Historic context: tribes and khans

Chinggis Khan was born during a turbulent period in Mongolia in late autumn of 1162 and given the name Temüjin. While Mongolia had been the home of several empires, such as the Xiongnu (circa 200 BCE-200 CE) and the Uighurs (744-840), and then became part of the Liao Empire (906-1125), during Temüjin's youth, it was a land divided among several tribal confederations, each vying for control of pastures as well as access to the trade routes of the historical silk roads. In 1162, the Mongols were but one confederation on the steppe. A few decades earlier, they had become a rising force. Indeed, their rapid emergence so concerned the Jin Empire in northern China and Manchuria that they aided the Tatars, a rival tribe, against the Mongols. The Tatars lured the Mongol khan Ambaghai into a trap and sent him as a prisoner to the Jin Emperor. There, Ambaghai was tortured and executed in an imaginative and humiliating way—nailed to a wooden donkey.

Why a donkey? Because the Mongols were steppe nomads who rode horses. Only sedentary cultures domesticated donkeys or rode them. Ambaghai's death therefore symbolically broke his nomadic spirit and transformed him into a sedentary farmer—the kind of lowly person who he himself might raid.

Ambaghai's death led to a number of consequences. Prior to his reign, the Mongols were led by Qabul Khan of the Borjigid Mongols. Although Qabul had seven sons, the khanship passed to Ambaghai of the Tayichi'ud Mongols, a different branch. While this was a major shift, it was not surprising, because while the position of khan could be hereditary, it was not necessarily so. In this book, I use the term tribe, which often makes scholars uncomfortable, as a lot of baggage can accompany it from its earlier use, which usually meant a group of people bonded by a common lineage to a real or fictional ancestor. The latter definition often falls apart on scrutiny. Now it is fashionable to use the term lineage to discuss the dominant elements of a steppe society or even use the indigenous term such as *oboq* and *yasu*. I, on the other hand, believe that the term "tribe" has some validity, as the average reader is at least familiar with it in a general sense. Furthermore, my use of tribe is guided by the definition of the term by Rudi Lindner in his classic article, "What was a Nomadic Tribe?"

To sum up, the medieval Eurasian nomadic tribe was a political organism open to all who were willing to subordinate themselves to its chief and who shared interests with its tribesmen. It was a dynamic organism that could expand or contract its fellowship in short order; its growth or decay was intimately related to the wisdom and success of its chief's actions. It derived its identity from its chief, a fact which implied that its continued and powerful existence over several generations was doubtful (Lindner, 701).

I would add the caveat that "chief" can be replaced by lineage, and most members of the larger tribe are not related to it through a real or fictive ancestor. We must accept the idea that the name of any "tribe" or "clan" comes from the dominant element in any group related to the primary lineage. Secondly, there was some common identity defined by region, language, lineage, ethnicity, culture or a combination of these.

Tribal identity was fluid. Groups could move in and out of the tribe—sometimes voluntarily, sometimes not. Tribes often grew by forcibly dominating weaker groups. Others sought the protection of a more powerful tribe against external threats. Nor were all members of a tribe equal to one another; instead, a hierarchy existed. Additionally, these tribes could be acephalous, meaning that there was not a single dominant leader, but several leading figures who conferred on decisions. At times, one figure might gain ascendancy over others, particularly in times of crisis when strong leadership was needed. Otherwise, the various groups tended to be largely autonomous. Among the tribes of Mongolia, the title for such a ruler was khan. However, once a man became khan, he was not guaranteed to remain as such. He was supported by a number of retainers (*nökörs*) or men bonded to him by loyalty. If the khan assisted them in maintaining their status through gifts, rewards, and privileges, these *nökörs* helped him. If he failed to do so, eventually they might seek employment elsewhere, or help someone else seize the throne. While one can view this kind of "betrayal" as self-serving, the *nökör* had valid concerns, just as stockholders or employees might with a CEO; if he or she is doing a fine job, then all is good. But if they are failing, then others will be affected as well. Of course, unlike lay-offs or declining dividends, failure on the steppes could mean death. A weak khan invited disaster. Conversely, although a strong khan was desirable, too much autocracy also risked disaster. The benefit of being a nomad was that you could vote with your feet (or hooves) and leave. There was always a risk of retaliation, but tribal confederations only worked well when a good khan listened to the needs of the subordinate leaders and upheld a just rule over the long term.

"Born amid the turmoil"

So what does this have to do with Temüjin's childhood? With Ambaghai's death, the Mongols now lacked a single leader while they were feuding with the Tatars. The Jin viewed the Mongols as neutered after the death of Ambaghai. They could be a nuisance, but no longer posed a threat. The Tatars, however, still had grudges to settle, and the Mongols reciprocated. Additionally, Ambaghai's death created an opportunity for the Borjigids to reclaim the leadership. Ultimately, the Mongols selected Qabul Khan's son Qutula as their khan. But despite engaging the Tatars in 13 encounters, the Mongols failed to defeat them and avenge Ambaghai's fate. After Qutula's death in the 1160s, no one could agree on a khan, so the Mongols became acephalous or, rather, polycephalous with one body. A Mongolian proverb says that once there were two snakes. One had a single body and many tails. The other had a single tail but many heads. As winter approached, they both sought places to hibernate for the winter. The first snake found one and quickly decided it was suitable. He entered it and survived the winter. The second snake found a promising hole, but the many heads each vied to enter first, as they all could not fit at once. Winter came, and the serpent died while still trying to establish claims of priority (Juvaini, 40-41). The Mongols had become like the second snake: they were not unified and slowly fractured.

Temüjin was born amid this turmoil in 1162, clutching a blood clot in his tiny fist; his name was chosen by his parents because his father, Yisügei, had recently captured a Tatar leader named Temüjin.

While naming your son after a prisoner captured on the same day as his birth might seem odd, the Mongols viewed it as an auspicious occasion. They may have hoped that part of the Tatar Temüjin's valor would transfer to the infant Temüjin—aided, of course, by executing the Tatar leader (Dunnell, *Chinggis Khan*, 21). Indeed, Yisügei was a minor leader among the Mongol confederation, although he appears to have been an up-and-coming chief, as he was one of the few Mongol leaders who experienced any military success against the Tatars. There is no indication that he was considered as khan, but due to his military talent, one cannot rule out the possibility that, in time, he might have ascended to the throne, especially since he was a grandson of Qabul Khan. His father was Bartan-ba'atur, Qabul's second son.

Temüjin's mother, Hö'elün, came from the Olqunu'ut, a subgroup of the Onggirad. She married Yisügei after he kidnapped her from her original husband, Yeke-Chiledü, a Merkit who lived just south of Lake Baikal. Abduction was not uncommon in the medieval steppes. Yisügei, however, was determined that Temüjin would not need to acquire a bride by the same method. When Temüjin was around the age of nine, his father took him to the Onggirad in search of a wife. This was not yet a marriage, but a betrothal, which would form the basis of a marriage alliance between the Borjigid Mongols of Yisügei and Temüjin's future wife and her people. Furthermore, the marriage could mend the gap between Yisügei and Hö'elün's family. Despite his success, Yisügei needed to be mindful that the Merkit or the Olqunu'ut could retaliate for his kidnapping of Hö'elün.

Temüjin, however, never reached the pastures of his mother's family. In route, he and his father encountered Dei Sechen, a leader of another branch of the Onggirad. Knowing the rising star of Yisügei, Dei Sechen convinced the Mongol leader that his daughter, Börte, would be the perfect match for young Temüjin. She was slightly older, and both beautiful and intelligent. Yisügei consented and left his son with Dei Sechen to become acquainted with his future father-in-law and fiancée.

On the return journey, however, Yisügei stopped at a camp for food and shelter—not an uncommon occurrence among nomads, then or now. Unfortunately, it was a Tatar camp, and they recognized Yisügei. Rather than attacking him outright, they poisoned his food instead. Thus, it was not until Yisügei departed that he became ill. Although he died shortly after returning to his own pastures and *ger* (or yurt), he sent someone to retrieve Temüjin. As they were still too young to be married, Börte remained with her father.

While it was quickly determined that the Tatars poisoned Yisügei, there was little a nine-year-old Temüjin could do. Yisügei's poisoning violated several steppe norms concerning hospitality for visitors. In the steppes, one could travel for days seeing no one. Thus, when someone came to one's camp, hospitality was expected and given—after all, you might need it one day as well. Food and shelter were imperative in a region where the winter temperature could reach 30 degrees below zero Fahrenheit, and where the open steppe offered little shelter from storms.

Yet Temüjin was not Yisügei's only surviving son. After him, Hö'elün gave birth to three more boys, Qasar, Qachi'un, Temüge, and then a daughter named Temülün. Two years in age separated all, making Temüjin nine, and Temülün perhaps one when their father died. As has been noted by others, the ages are neat and tidy. Temüjin's age itself is symbolic, as nine is an auspicious number. Yet, the two-year spacing is not incongruous with breastfeeding, which is thought to stop the woman from ovulating. After the mother weaned the child, she began ovulating again; thus, the timing of Hö'elün's children was not out of the ordinary. Yisügei also had another wife named Suchigil, who produced two sons. Bekter was older than Temüjin, while Belgütei was younger, perhaps even younger than Qasar. Still, all were young, and not in any position to lead the Mongols or avenge Yisügei's death.

As a rising war leader, Yisügei had attracted a following. Warriors will follow leaders who increase their chances of victory and thus loot, as regular paychecks did not exist. While risking one's life for vengeance is all well and good, it doesn't lead to a comfortable life. The need to acquire goods was important. For Temüjin's family, therefore, Yisügei's untimely death meant a loss of status. This was most apparent at a *quriltai* that occurred not long afterwards.

Quriltais (a congress or massive meeting) were infrequently held, as they required that all the factions involved gathered in one location. Since nomads traveled with their herds of horses, oxen or yaks, camels, and flocks of sheep and goats, holding a *quriltai* also meant finding a location that had sufficient pasture for thousands of animals for several days. Thus, they were only held for major events and ceremonies. While Yisügei had been a rising star among the Borjigid Mongols, another branch known as the Tayichi'ud saw his death as an opportunity to regain the reins of leadership. As no khan existed since Qutula Khan died (the year is uncertain), the events that followed are connected to the absence of a khan and perhaps the *quriltai* was held in order to determine a new khan. While one did not emerge from the *quriltai*, other events occurred. The widows of Ambaghai Khan, Örbei and Soqatai excluded Hö'elün from participating in the ancestral rites. Why no one interceded is unclear, but this may have been because of the absence of a khan who could enforce societal norms and prevent the fraying of the fabric of the community.

When the *quriltai* ended, the Tayichi'ud attempted to coerce most of Yisügei's followers to depart with them, even killing the elderly Charaqa, one of Yisügei's *nökörs* who interfered. Hö'elün briefly rallied some of them by riding with Yisügei's standard and shaming them for their desertion. Hidden from Hö'elün's gaze under the cover of night, they abandoned the widow. *The Secret History of the Mongols*, our only detailed contemporary Mongolian source on Chinggis Khan, emphasizes that Temüjin's family was abandoned. One must question whether this is accurate, as they had spotted others in their company besides immediate family members. Nonetheless, the ostracization of Yisügei's family was tantamount to a death sentence on the cold and unforgiving steppe, where the weak became prey to the more powerful.

The situation worsened. Driven to dire straits and deprived of most of their herds and flocks, which the Tayichi'ud also took, Hö'elün and her family survived by finding wild vegetables, berries, fishing (something only done through necessity among the nomads), and hunting. Their scant food was shared and barely sufficient to feed them. During this period of trials, Hö'elün reminded the children of the "Parable of the Five Arrows," which concerned Alan Qoa, an ancestress of the Mongols, and her five sons. Two were from her husband, and three were born after his death from a heavenly figure. Because of their uncertain parentage and absence of a father, the children often quarreled. During the times of difficulty, Alan Qoa told her sons they needed to be unified and demonstrated this by giving each of them an arrow to break. They did so easily. She then gave them a bundle of arrows. None of them could break it. She instructed them that they were all like the arrows—individually they were weak, but if they remained unified, no one could break them (SHM, §19, 76). With flagrant disregard for Hö'elün's lesson, Bekter hoarded food and stole game from Temüjin and Jochi Qasar. As a result, Temüjin and his brother then murdered their elder half-brother. A livid Hö'elün berated her children, calling them destroyers and reminding them, "Apart from our shadows, we have no friends:" (SHM, §77). The sources do not reveal Suchigil's reaction. Belgütei, however, was spared at Bekter's request.

Most curious is that neither Hö'elün nor Suchigil remarried immediately. Among the Mongols, the custom of Levirate marriage existed. It was not uncommon for a widow to marry her husband's brother or another relative. Yisügei had brothers—indeed, they assisted Yisügei when he abducted Hö'elün. One was still alive yet curiously, he does not enter the picture during this troubling period. Yet, the Levirate marriage still could happen. If a brother did not marry the wife, then it was also possible for her to marry one of her stepsons. Bekter was a couple of years older than Temüjin. It is uncertain when Temüjin murdered Bekter, but some scholars have hypothesized that the murder may have had to do with this possibility (Weatherford, 2004, 23-24; Dunnell 2010, 24). While Bekter's theft of food hurt the family and threatened their well-being, it still seems like a considerable escalation to murder him for it. While it appears unlikely that a marriage between Bekter and Hö'elün would have restored the good fortunes of the family, it might have established some sense of normalcy and allowed them to return to the fold. In the end, it did not matter, since the murder did not go unnoticed.

Before long, the Tayichi'ud captured Temüjin. It is usually assumed that this was a punishment for the murder of Bekter. Yet, if Temüjin's family had been abandoned, then why did it matter? We must consider that the family was not completely ostracized, but rather reduced in status, which meant that violations of customs, such as murder, still mattered. While the Tayichi'ud may have contemplated executing Temüjin, they ultimately enslaved him instead. To feed and maintain him, the Tayichi'ud passed Temüjin from Tayichi'ud commoner household to household, many of which included Yisügei's former supporters. One also gets the sense that the welfare of the commoner households was based on their care of Temüjin—not only feeding him, but also ensuring that he didn't escape. Undoubtedly, it also served as a reminder of misfortunes that befell Yisügei's family. While Temüjin undoubtedly worked around the camp as a slave, spending an indeterminate time as a captive there, he also spent time in a cangue, a yoke-like restraining device that made sleep or the use of one's hands difficult. Some of the lower-class took pity and released him from the cangue at night so he could at least sleep comfortably and tend to his chafing sores caused by the device.

One day, during a celebration, Temüjin escaped. He cleverly used his cangue to knock out his inattentive guard, and then hid in a stream, now using the cangue as a flotation device. The Tayichi'ud searched for him, and a commoner name Sorqan Shira found him, but Sorqan Shira craftily directed the search elsewhere. Later, Temüjin took refuge in Sorqan Shira's tent. His family had been kind to Temüjin before, removing the cangue at night. They were a commoner family of no standing, but also formerly part of Yisügei's camp, and thus shared some emotional familiarity with

Temüjin. Now they released him from the cangue, burned it in the fire, thus destroying the evidence of his presence, and then hid him in a cart of wool while the Tayichi'ud's search continued. Temüjin narrowly escaped recapture, which would have also implicated Sorqan Shira's family. When it came time for him to flee the Tayichi'ud camp, Sorqan Shira provided him with a horse, some food, and a bow with a few arrows—enough to hunt and perhaps defend himself, but insufficient for anything foolish.

A generous man

After a successful escape, Temüjin rejoined his family. Curiously, the Tayichi'ud did not pursue him. No reason is given, yet one suspects that it may have something to do with the fact that the Mongols remained divided without a khan. Or, perhaps the Tayichi'ud reasoned, he had served his time and found a way to escape, thus earning his liberty. Yet, his childhood hostilities with the Tayichi'ud were not finished. At some point, some Tayichi'ud stole his family's horses. Only one horse remained, which Belgütei rode while out hunting. When he returned, Temüjin took that horse in pursuit of the thieves. While in pursuit, he came across another youth named Bo'orchu milking his father's mares. This in itself was not unusual—milking mares was considered "men's work". What was unusual was that Bo'orchu had indeed seen horse thieves pass by, but they did not touch his horses. This indicates that Bo'orchu was not just a common nomad, but that his father, Naqu-Bayan (Naqu the rich), was probably a man of some stature, thus deterring ordinary rustlers. Indeed, Naqu-Bayan and Bo'orchu were of the Arulat, a Mongol group associated with Borjigids. Thus, while the thieves may have been Tayichi'ud, we should not ascribe this to some conspiracy against Temüjin, but rather a crime of opportunity.

Bo'orchu joined Temüjin in his pursuit and helped him regain the horses. Temüjin then offered half of them to Bo'orchu as a reward. Bo'orchu declined as he already had so much, and Temüjin so little. This moment in Temüjin's life was a culmination of events. First, his offer of half of the "plunder" (i.e. his own horses), demonstrates a generosity and appreciation of assistance and loyalty that became a hallmark of Chinggis Khan's career. One must remember that while in the Tayichi'ud camp, Temüjin was not housed with the rich and powerful, but with the commoners. He had thus experienced not only dire circumstances with his own family, but also the life of a commoner. Through this, he became familiar with many different circumstances of status. While he was born an aristocrat, he also understood the life from the bottom of the hierarchy. The offer of half of the loot was generous and somewhat expected, but Bo'orchu's refusal was based on the fact that he had assisted Temüjin out of a desire to help, not out of any obligation or with the expectation of reward. Indeed, Naqu-bayan, Bo'orchu's father, insisted that Bo'orchu go with Temüjin and they be companions (SHM, §93). This also makes one suspicious that Temüjin was perhaps not as isolated as the sources want us to believe. Why would a father of some standing want his son to join some guy who can't even keep his own horses? Bo'orchu did not join Temüjin immediately, but would do so soon.

Not long after this adventure, Temüjin decided to marry, probably in 1177, when he would have been around 15—now a man. He had not forgotten his betrothal to Börte. Surprisingly, neither had Dei Sechen, Börte's father, who was well informed of Temüjin's trials and travails. Not only did he permit the marriage to go forward, but also he and his wife, Chotan, accompanied the newlyweds part of the way back to Temüjin's camp, perhaps to ensure someone did not kidnap Börte. Chotan continued with her daughter to Temüjin's camp by the Senggür stream. Although Chotan eventually returned home, before she did so, she gave Hö'elün a sumptuous and valuable gift—a black sable coat. At the same time, Temüjin sent Belgütei to request Bo'orchu to join him. With his marriage and the arrival of Bo'orchu, we see Temüjin entering his manhood and assuming the reins of leadership among his family. Bo'orchu appears to be his first *nökör* or companion. Temüjin and Börte were also now in a position to start their own family, yet they still needed additional security.

With Bo'orchu now in his camp, Temüjin, Qasar, and Belgütei took the sable coat and rode to the Tula River, where Toghril, Khan of the powerful Kereit confederation, dwelled. Yisügei and Toghril had been *anda*, a "sworn brotherhood," similar to being blood brothers. This differed from being a *nökör*, as the latter implied an unequal relationship where the *nökör* was subordinate to another. In an *anda* relationship, the two were equals. Using this tie, Temüjin then presented the sable coat to Toghril as a gift. By accepting it, Toghril acknowledged Temüjin and took him as a *nökör*. He promised to assist Temüjin in gathering his people.

This was a crucial move. By assuming the mantle of leadership of his family, Temüjin needed protection, and thus a patron. One can question why Toghril, a powerful figure who dominated central Mongolia, would even take Temüjin into his fold, but the reasons are simple. In doing so, he showed respect to his former *anda*. Temüjin may have also played on Toghril's guilt for not assisting his *anda*'s family after Yisügei's death. After all, Yisügei had helped Toghril gain and keep his throne. On the surface, Toghril risked little by taking Temüjin as a *nökör*. He was small potatoes, so to speak. Toghril also gained a valuable sable coat and could help Temüjin gather his people in due time. Although Temüjin was a Borjigid Mongol, not a Kereit, it was not unusual for the leader of a group to attach himself to a larger tribe, such as the Kereit. It is possible that Temüjin also spent some time in Toghril's court during Yisügei's lifetime, which may have given Toghril a sentimental attachment to the young man. As an insignificant player in the world of the steppe, Temüjin needed ties to a stronger entity, as it was clear that other Mongols would not necessarily aid him. Yet, we should not think of Temüjin's following as consisting simply of his brothers and Bo'orchu, since Bo'orchu most likely brought men with him as well. It is also likely that Temüjin's family still had some people attached to them. Still, the numbers were probably small—a few dozen or so.

At this time, Temüjin was entering not only the world of manhood, but also that of leadership among the Mongols. Nevertheless, in 1182 he was still very far from being Chinggis Khan.

2. Chinggis Khan as Temüjin (1182—1187)

This chapter is titled "Chinggis Khan as Temüjin" as it explores the life of Temüjin before he became Chinggis Khan and how Temüjin transformed into the historical figure known as Chinggis Khan. While it is popularly assumed that Temüjin sought to unify the steppes, it is not quite that simple. Clearly, Temüjin had an agenda, but it was one that I think many people can relate to: surviving and restoring his family's fortunes. His path was not straight, but with many curves and forks on the road. There was nothing inevitable about Temüjin's rise to power. It required hard work, copious amounts of good luck, and of course learning from his mistakes.

At this time, Temüjin's greatest concern must have been the Tayichi'ud. Although Temüjin became Toghril's *nökör* by giving him the sable coat, the gift did not mean that Toghril blanketed his new protégé with protection. As was usual, Temüjin stayed in his own pastures, near the Kerülen River, since moving too close to the Kereit could strain Toghril's pastures. Furthermore, by remaining in the Onan-Kerülen basin, Temüjin extended Toghril's influence east. During this time, an old blacksmith of the Uriangqai tribe, named Jarchi'udai came with his young son, Jelme. Jarchi'udai had been a member of Yisügei's camp and now came to Temüjin. Furthermore, Jarchi'udai gave Jelme to Temüjin to be his servant. While an innocuous moment, Jelme had a bright future, but it also showed that Temüjin was slowly "getting the band back together," as it were. Yisügei's people were slowly filtering back to him.

Temüjin's stability proved ephemeral, however, when the Merkit finally avenged the abduction of Hö'elün decades earlier. A raiding party, which Temüjin's family at first wrongly assumed were Tayichi'ud, struck Temüjin's camp and absconded with Börte as well as Suchigil. Meanwhile, Temüjin and the rest of his family escaped, evading certain destruction. This was not a simple hit-and-run raid, but one targeted to avenge Hö'elün's kidnapping by Yisügei. Her initial husband, Chiledü, clearly had neither forgotten nor forgiven the trespass. He had, however, been powerless to do much. Indeed, at the time of Hö'elün's kidnapping, she clearly saw that Chiledü would not survive the encounter and urged him to flee, saying, "If only you are spared, you will always find a girl or woman like me. If her name is different, name her also, Hö'elün. Save your life! Never forget to breathe my scent!" (SHM, §55). She then literally gave him the shirt off her back so he had something to remember her by, which naturally also carried her scent, a powerful trigger for memories (Weatherford 2004, 12). Chiledü fled for his life. It is apparent that genuine affection existed between the two. To our knowledge, however, Hö'elün never attempted to return to the Merkit, even after Yisügei's death. Indeed, considering her five children from Yisügei, it is unlikely they would have been accepted, even considering the fluid nature of tribes.

This raid may have sought to eliminate Yisügei's seed, while also taking Temüjin's new wife. The timing of the raid makes it clear the Merkit had learned that Yisügei's eldest son had taken a wife, thus opening the door for vengeance. Even though they captured Börte as she tried to escape in an ox-drawn *ger*—not the fastest of getaway vehicles, but the only one available—the Merkit still pursued the fleeing Temüjin and only gave up after they lost him in the dense forests of Mount Burqan-Qaldun. Temüjin was so thankful for the mountain that sheltered him, that he later made it a protected area, essentially a nature preserve; he also prayed to the mountain spirit and offered sacrifices to it. Meanwhile, the Merkit married Börte to Chilger-Bökö, Chiledü's younger brother.

Unlike the Merkit, Temüjin did not wait almost two decades for vengeance. As a *nökör*, he went to Toghril and requested his assistance, which Toghril gave freely, not only because Temüjin was his *nökör*, but also because Toghril himself felt a long-standing animosity towards the Merkit who had enslaved him during his childhood. In addition to gaining Toghril's aid, Temüjin became reacquainted with a childhood friend and *anda*, Jamuqa. Jamuqa and Temüjin had become *anda* to one another at age 11. Unlike Temüjin's difficulties, Jamuqa life appears to have taken another path. It is strange that Jamuqa seems to have been absent from Temüjin's life, although perhaps, as a child, what could he have done to help? Now Jamuqa was not only the leader of the Jadaran Mongols (another branch, separate from the Borjigid and Tayichi'ud), but he was Toghril's war leader as well. In his current capacity, Jamuqa served Toghril and could muster two *tümens* or 20,000 men, if we assume the numbers are correct and the *tümen* were at full strength. From this, we can take it that as Toghril brought two *tümen* and Jamuqa brought two, they had a sizeable army, regardless of precise numbers.

Their attack was not a complete surprise. The army of retribution entered Merkit territory by crossing the Kilqo River, which was sufficiently strong and deep that they had to build rafts to cross it. Sentries as well as hunters and fishermen spotted the invaders' flotilla and warned the Merkit prior to the triumvirate's arrival (A triumvirate is a group of three people working together). However, the Merkit did not prevail or escape Temüjin's wrath. With Toghril and Jamuqa's aid, Temüjin successfully recovered Börte, albeit months after her abduction. While Temüjin did not take years, a rescue operation into enemy territory was not as simple as getting a posse together and riding in hot pursuit. Suchigil, however, never returned. During the raid, she fled into the Siberian forests, even as her son Belgütei searched for her. Whereas Börte married Chilger-Bökö, a Merkit aristocrat, the much older Suchigil was given to a commoner. This disgrace proved too much for the once-proud wife of Yisügei and she remained with the Merkit, never to return to her distraught son. Chilger, however, proved equally fleet of foot as his brother was years ago and escaped. Meanwhile, the victors rounded up the Merkit women they captured and returned home with their new concubines and wives, not to mention copious amounts of loot.

With their victory, Temüjin remained with Jamuqa for several months, renewing their friendship by exchanging gifts taken from the Merkit plunder. Temüjin also received a gift from Börte, his first son. At the time of her rescue, Börte was pregnant with her second child and first son, Jochi. This son, Jochi, was born in Jamuqa's camp. The word "Jochi" means guest, which might refer to his birth in Jamuqa's camp. Alternatively, it could indicate that he was a guest in Temüjin's family, alluding to the possibility that Börte had indeed been impregnated by the Merkit Chilger-Bökö, not Temüjin. While Temüjin does not appear to have ever questioned the paternity of the child, it became an issue later. This event raises several interesting issues.

Clearly, Börte had been abandoned by Temüjin during the attack. As with Chiledü, Temüjin and company quickly determined they were outnumbered and embraced the idea that the better part of valor was living to fight another day. It was not as if an unmarked van pulled up and masked men grabbed Börte while she was strolling down a sidewalk, but a sizeable force of dozens, if not hundreds, thundering across the steppe abducted her. Not only did the men flee, but also Hö'elün. Couldn't someone grab Börte? Perhaps not. Another factor might have been a child. Jochi was Temüjin and Börte's first son, but their second child. Their first child was Qojin, who was not mentioned in the sources for this scenario. We do not know what happened to her. Was she abducted, too? Did grandma Hö'elün or someone else grab her, or was Hö'elün encumbered with Temülün, Temüjin's young sister? Qojin was still a toddler and thus easy to carry on a horse. It is unlikely one of the men did—holding a child while riding a horse and potentially shooting arrows would be a difficult endeavor even for a medieval Mongol. Also, the event took place early in the morning. It is quite possible that Börte may have still been feeding Qojin or dealing with other issues associated with a toddler. While rumors would later spawn that Jochi was a Merkit bastard, it is also possible that Börte was pregnant and could not easily mount or ride a horse and thus had to escape in an oxcart driven by a servant.

An "apprenticeship of sorts"

Jamuqa and Temüjin's reunion lasted for approximately a year and a half, but eventually Temüjin, upon the advice of Börte, separated from Jamuqa. While their time together was brief, it proved important, as it served as not only a reunion, but also an apprenticeship of sorts for Temüjin. As his father died in Temüjin's youth, Temüjin had little experience leading, particularly in war. Although he had taken part in the attack on the Merkit, there is no indication that he commanded any aspect of it. It was therefore time well spent, as Jamuqa proved to be a talented war leader. Leading in battle, however, requires a different set of skills than in times of peace, as Temüjin discovered when he departed from Jamuqa.

Their separation was unusual, and the passage concerning it was cryptic, even to Temüjin at the time. As they migrated to a new pasture and made preparation to camp, Jamuqa said,

> Let us camp near the mount:
> There will be enough shelter
> For our horse-herders!
> Let us camp near the river:
> There will be enough food
> For our shepherds and lamb-herds! (SHM, §118)

The meanings of these words baffled Temüjin. This might be viewed as a commentary on social class, differentiating between Jamuqa and Temüjin (Ratchnevsky, 37-38). While there might be some validity to this interpretation, I am hesitant to subscribe to a Marxist interpretation of a class struggle between aristocratic horse-breeders and common shepherds based on a comment made by a medieval steppe nomad who needed multiple types of livestock in order to survive in the steppes. Furthermore, both men were upper class. Although the Borjigid lineage had more prestige, Jamuqa, as leader of the Jadaran, still carried ample respect, particularly because of his own merit. While Ruth Dunnell dismisses the class distinction, she considers that Jamuqa speaks more from the tribal elder's position to Temüjin's more junior position, which is reasonable. As Igor de Rachewiltz indicates, the statement is simply practical—the animals must be pastured in different areas. (Rachewiltz, 441) This in itself is not what puzzled Temüjin; as someone who grew up in the steppe, he would have had a grasp on the proper way to pasture the livestock in which the animals graze grass differently. Both Dunnell and Rachewiltz agree that the issue is how Jamuqa said the otherwise innocuous statement. Unable to decipher Jamuqa's intent, Temüjin waited for the cart that carried the one person whose advice he had always valued—his mother. Thus he related Jamuqa's statement, but before Hö'elün could speak, Börte interjected, stating, "Sworn friend Jamuqa, so they say, grows *easily* tired *of his friends.* Now the time has come when he has grown tired of us … let us separate completely from him and move *further* on, travelling at night!" (SHM, §118)

Börte's reaction is significant. It marks a transition between Temüjin and his mother. While Hö'elün continued to be a valued counselor, Börte emerged as a more significant actor in the affairs of Temüjin's life. Indeed, she became his key advisor and active participant in his fate. Her purpose in this situation also served another role. By having her tell Temüjin that he should separate from Jamuqa, she became the tool for their split, shifting blame away from Temüjin for what we might view as poor behavior towards his *anda.* Rachewiltz is in agreement with this and believes the scenario is apocryphal and simply to justify actions taken to by Temüjin to emerge from his *anda's* shadow. One must also consider that maybe Börte was tired of being with Jamuqa. The *Secret History* indicates that her husband spent much of his time with his *anda* and that Jamuqa and Temüjin even slept under the same blanket. While it is tempting to speculate on some sort of sexual relationship, it is unlikely, and intended to mean they were like brothers; Temüjin slept in Jamuqa's tent, crashing on his couch, if you will. It is clear, however, that Temüjin spent more time carousing and drinking with his buddy Jamuqa than he did with his wife and children, particularly as Börte had recently given birth and may not have been in the mood for amorous advances. Regarding the separation from Jamuqa, while we must not dismiss Temüjin's own ambition, surely Börte also had her own interest in removing Temüjin from his *anda*'s influence, and not necessarily simply out of petty jealousy, although jealousy should not be completely discounted. Whether her dispensing of wisdom was apocryphal or simply a literary device used by the Secret Historian, her role as Temüjin's advisor is now apparent.

Elevated status

Temüjin's departure was, however, quite different from when he joined Jamuqa with only a handful of followers. While his followers accompanied his departure, Temüjin found his status increasing as several other people also joined him, including some of his relatives, who had previously attached themselves to Jamuqa's retinue. Additionally, many commoners also departed the Jadaran camp. It is important to remember that a "tribe" took its identity from the leading lineages, but its structure was fluid. When a leader ceased to be effective (for whatever reason), members might leave. It was up to the tribal leader to provide an incentive for members to stay. A khan could only rule as an autocrat if he had sufficient military power to enforce his will. Even then, ensuring the satisfaction of the military component limited the khan's autocracy. To rule as a khan, one needed to listen and keep his subordinate leaders, including his *nökörs*, happy, or they would find a new leader to follow. After the Merkit raid, Temüjin was more generous than Jamuqa in distributing the plunder—something that did not escape notice. In the 18 months that Jamuqa and Temüjin stayed together, others probably noted other aspects of Temüjin that they found more appealing—some positive and some negative.

Temüjin was bewildered by the show of support, or perhaps a

preference for him, over Jamuqa. One individual who joined him, for example, explained that he had a dream in which,

> We would not have parted from him, but a *heavenly sign* appeared before my *very* eyes, revealing *the future to me*. There came a fallow cow. She circled Jamuqa and struck his tent-cart with her horns; *then* she butted him *too*, breaking one of her two horns. Being *thus left* with uneven horns, 'Bring me my horn!' she kept saying, bellowing repeatedly at Jamuqa as she stood there, *hoofing up the ground and* raising more and more dust. Then a hornless and fallow ox lifted up the great shaft under the tent, harnessed it on to himself and pulled it after him. As he proceeded following Temüjin on the wide road, he kept bellowing, 'Together Heaven and Earth have agreed: Temüjin shall be lord of the People! (SHM, §121)

With such a portent, how could Temüjin refuse the support of these new followers? The mass defection of both aristocrats and commoners, however, suggests that while Jamuqa was a talented war leader, they found his leadership in other situations lacking. Furthermore, although Jamuqa was the leader of the Jadaran, the Jadaran lacked the prestige of the Borjigid lineage. The Borjigids were descended from Bodonchar, one of the three heavenly sons of Alan Qoa, the ancestress who told the "Parable of the Arrows" to her children, while the Jadaran were descended only from an adopted son of Bodonchar, and thus did not have a direct link to Alan Qoa or the heavenly ancestor.

So great was the support for Temüjin that his backers convened a small *quriltai* in 1185 and agreed to make Temüjin the khan of the Borjigid Mongols. Although *The Secret History of the Mongols* indicates that he also received the title of Chinggis Khan, it is unlikely that he did so. Rather, the *Secret History* added the anachronism to further legitimize Chinggis Khan's stature. Indeed, it is likely his uncles and other more senior Mongols elevated him to the throne, as they believed that his relative youth (he was approximately 23 years old) and inexperience would make him malleable and prevent a violent struggle among them over the title of khan. The young Temüjin does not fit our historic image of the resolute and intimidating figure of Chinggis Khan. Thus, while his relatives made stylized oaths of loyalty, they may not have been sincere. Temüjin's selection not only removed potential conflict among the other Borjigids, but it also allowed them to restore the title of khan to the Borjigid line, and therefore bypassing the Tayichi'ud claims. Of course, this also meant that the Tayichi'ud did not recognize his legitimacy. Jamuqa also still led the Jadaran Mongols. When Temüjin broke away from Jamuqa, he passed near a Tayichi'ud camp, causing them to panic and flee to Jamuqa. While the *Secret History* does not mention that Temüjin engaged in violence in the Tayichi'ud camp, it is likely that the Borjigid Mongols pillaged their camp rather than simply investigate the empty tents. With the Tayichi'ud now under the protection of Jamuqa of the Jadaran, they could not possibly claim the title of khan, as the Tayichi'ud were also descended from the heavenly sons of Alan Qoa. By placing themselves under Jamuqa's protection, they lacked the legitimacy to proclaim a khan. Indeed, one might surmise that Temüjin's relatives, who had been in Jamuqa's camp, may have acknowledged a similar situation for themselves and viewed the up-and-coming Temüjin as a pliable dupe, conspiring to have him break with his *anda*. With sufficient encouragement, he did so and departed with a sizeable following. Although we may never know the full story, there was enough suspicious activity to make it clear that his relatives did not make him khan simply because of his plucky character and that he polled well among dream cattle.

While both Toghril and Jamuqa sent congratulatory messages to Temüjin, tensions simmered beneath the surface. As part of the message, Jamuqa also chided Altan and Quchar, two of Temüjin's relatives (Altan was Qutula Khan's son), "Why did you not make sworn friend Temüjin *qan* (sic) when we were *still* together—without causing the sworn friend and me to fall apart? Just what did you have in mind now, when you made him *qan* (sic)?" (SHM,

§127) Jamuqa clearly thought the selection of Temüjin as khan was based on ulterior motives and that Jamuqa was bitter that this process took place only after they left him, implying that they never considered Jamuqa as a potential khan.

Before long, Jamuqa and Temüjin came into conflict. The trouble began after Jamuqa's younger relative, Taichar, was killed while stealing horses from Jochi-darmala, one of Temüjin's *nökörs*. Angry, Jamuqa gathered the Jadaran and the other groups associated with him, which undoubtedly included the Tayichi'ud, to seek vengeance. Temüjin soon learned of Jamuqa's intent and gathered his own forces. No arbitration efforts took place. While a feud could result from a death like Taichar's, assembling an army of perhaps 30,000 men seems like overkill. Stealing horses and other livestock was not unusual, nor was getting killed. Rather, a death such as this resulted either in a tit-for-tat exchange or an agreed amount of compensation, or perhaps even the intervention of another to render judgment, such as their suzerain, Toghril.

In order for Toghril to intercede, he would have needed to be present, but by this point, Toghril lost his own throne to his brother, Jaqa Gambu, or a relative named Erke Qara—the events are muddled. Exactly when this occurred is difficult to pinpoint, but it occurred sometime between Börte's rescue (1184), in which Toghril and Jaqa Gambu took part, and the Battle of Dalan Baljut (1187). Toghril fled first to Qara Khitai (in present-day Kyrgyzstan and southern Kazakhstan), and then eventually took refuge in the kingdom of Xi Xia (currently Gansu and Ningxia provinces of the People's Republic of China), southwest of Mongolia. The kingdom of Xi Xia had close ties with the Kereit, and indeed Jaqa Gambu had lived in Xi Xia before returning to the Kereit in the early 1180s. A scholar, Isenbike Togan, suggests that Temüjin's elevation to khan took place during Toghril's absence, since surely this action, which gave Temüjin a title on par with Toghril's, would have alarmed the Kereit khan, particularly when Temüjin was not even supported by most of the Mongols. (Togan, 82-83) Temüjin may have even become *anda* with Jaqa Gambu, swaying with the winds of change.

The events at Dalan Baljut demonstrate, however, that if Temüjin now supported Jaqa Gambu, Jamuqa probably did not, and that Jaqa Gambu's patronage and protection was unsteady at best, as he seems to have been forced to flee to Jin territory, most likely due to the rise of Erke Qara.

Thus, there were two reasons to start a war. While Taichar's death may have been personal to Jamuqa, it is surprising that others aligned with Jamuqa would have gambled on an open battle just to avenge Taichar's death. Major battles were risky propositions, and the fate of kingdoms (or tribal confederations) could hinge on the result. Jamuqa's actions were not based on emotion, but on calculation. Temüjin may have been khan, but he lacked Jamuqa's considerable experience leading armies and commanding battles, while this would be Temüjin's first battle as a general.

Another option suggests that Temüjin started the conflict at the urging of his relatives to unify the Mongol people by defeating his now rival, Jamuqa. The resulting battle between Temüjin and Jamuqa in the narrow defile at Dalan-Baljut in 1187 led to Temüjin's defeat and mysterious disappearance. There is an approximate 10-year gap in the sources before Temüjin reappeared in Mongolia. Some evidence suggests that after his defeat, Temüjin went to the Jin Empire, but in what capacity (refugee, slave, soldier?) remains uncertain. (MDBL, 49)

3. The Rise of Chinggis Khan (1196-1206)

Temüjin returned to Mongolia around 1196-97, and apparently resumed where he left off. The *Secret History* is silent on his absence and simply moved from the defeat at Dalan Baljut to the next event in Mongolia, a battle with the Tatars. Thus, Temüjin did not suffer any ill consequences of his defeat, and the scrappy Mongol leader was once again the khan of the Borjigid Mongols and a *nökör*, or perhaps even *anda*, of Toghril, despite his relationship with Jaqa Gambu. Considering the fluctuations of leadership in the steppe, those in power could not view transfers of allegiance as acts of duplicity but just as part of life. Temüjin, however, quickly proved that he was no longer the inexperienced leader and dupe that his relatives had manipulated for their own purposes.

Based on his actions, we can gather that he gained valuable lessons while outside of Mongolia. It is reasonable to assume that Temüjin spent time in the Jin Empire. As Dalan Baljut is near the Onan River in northeastern Mongolia, the Jin frontier in Manchuria was not far away. In defeat, Temüjin may have also headed south towards the Jin frontier, perhaps crossing the Gobi Desert and taking refuge in what is now the Inner Mongolia Autonomous Region of China, or heading east into Manchuria. Unlike the Kereit, the Mongols did not have ties to Xi Xia, which was also considerably farther away from the Mongols' traditional pastures in the Onan-Kerulen basin, and so it is unlikely that Temüjin fled there for refuge.

The scholar Isenbike Togan suggests that perhaps Temüjin was captured while raiding the Jin frontier (Togan, 85). It is a possibility. Considering the next events to unfold, I would say that Temüjin was not simply captured, but he entered Jin service (perhaps not by choice) as one of the *jüyin*, a term used by the Jin to refer to the frontier groups (nomads and sedentary) who served as border guards and "trip wires" to prevent invasion from the steppes. The *jüyin* also allowed the Jin to extend their influence into the steppes. This, in my mind, is confirmed by the Mongol attack on the Tatars, discussed below.

The Tatars had themselves served in this *jüyin* capacity during the halcyon days of the Mongol khan, Qabul. They had been instrumental in the Jin victory over the Mongols in the 1160s, but with the shattering of the Mongols as well as Toghril's overthrow, the resultant power vacuum allowed the Tatars to grow incrementally in power. By the mid-1190s, they had transformed from complacent clients to rapacious raiders no longer content to be vassals of the Jin protecting the frontier, especially when the Jin gave them less than their fair share of plunder after a raid in 1195 on the Onggirad near the Jin frontier. As a result, the Jin, sought to nip their *jüyins* behavior in the bud.

Toghril had also returned to power. How they did this remains unclear, but Temüjin appears to have been involved, perhaps in league with the Jin. Temüjin seems to have even raided the Merkit to acquire material support (animals, people, and equipment) for Toghril. Additionally, Temüjin brought Jaqa Gambu with him. While Rashid al-Din says Temüjin rescued him from the Jin Empire, the events that unfolded make clear that this was not a daring rescue but rather because of the Jin machinations (JT, 388). It is at least clear that Temüjin's relationship with his former patron, Toghril, was now quite different. While Temüjin may have been a *nökör*, it appears that they acted more as equals rather than liege and vassal, and perhaps even *anda*. Regardless, Toghril returned as the khan of the Kereit in either 1196 or 1197. The timing is uncertain and thus affects the next event, because if Toghril returned in 1197, then he may not have taken part in the campaign against the Tatars.

In any case, the Mongols and the Kereit (led by either Jaqa Gambu or Toghril) joined forces with the Jin Empire against the Tatars. The Tatars comprised several tribes, but Temüjin and Toghril's victory over them rendered a portion of them impotent. As a result, the

Jin bestowed Toghril with the title of *wang* or king, formally recognizing him as a figure of some stature. Here we again have the question of when this occurred. If Toghril participated, then he could not have received the title as the Jin commander Wanyen Xiang lacked the authority to grant the title of wang; only the emperor could do this. Yet, at some point in 1196 or 1197, Toghril received the title, indicating that the Kereit leader fit in the larger picture of Jin steppe strategy.

Temüjin also received a title, *jaut qori*, meaning leader of a military unit (and not necessarily a high-ranking one), which again suggests that the Jin viewed Temüjin as a client. The Jin commander on the expedition also informed Temüjin he would petition the emperor to bestow upon Temüjin the more prestigious honorific title of *jeutau*, which translates formally as "Imperial Commissioner in Charge of Submitting and Punishing Rebels" or loosely as "barbarian-subduing generalissimo," both of which look nice on a business card. For studying Chinggis Khan, the difference in titles also shows that Toghril remained the more powerful, as well as the more respected leader, at least from the perspective of the Jin. Indeed, they may have felt that with Toghril, their "man in Mongolia", all would be well. For several years, this hope rang true as no tribal confederation in Mongolia posed a serious threat to the frontier. Indeed, until 1202 both Toghril and Temüjin often wintered near the long walls along the Jin border in what is now the Inner Mongolia Autonomous Region in the People's Republic of China.

We should not misconstrue these walls as the Great Wall of China, as the latter was not constructed—albeit it included sections of previous walls—until the Ming Dynasty (1368-1644), when construction began in 1474. For our intrepid nomads, their proximity confirms their ties to the Jin Empire. Their position by the walls during the winter also provided access to frontier market towns. They built the walls along strategic points to control access from Jin territory to the steppe, not only as defensive structures against the nomads (who could always find ways around), but also to control who went from the empire into the steppe and vice versa. No tax-collecting bureaucrat wanted smugglers or good tax-paying peasants to enjoy unfettered access to the relative freedom of the open steppe.

Despite the success of the campaign, the Jin Emperor, or Altan Khan (Golden King), as the nomads called him, did not hand out titles freely; there were always strings attached. The Jin Empire undoubtedly orchestrated Temüjin's return to Mongolia. As we don't know how Temüjin spent his time in the Jin Empire, we can only speculate that after his defeat by Jamuqa, the Jin welcomed him. It cost them little to keep him (or other princely refugees) in their pocket, knowing that he might someday be of use to them. In return for supporting his return to Mongolia in 1196, the Jin eliminated the Tatar threat to the empire. Furthermore, the Kereit and Temüjin's Mongols undoubtedly paid tribute to the Jin. Indeed, there is evidence that Chinggis Khan paid tribute until approximately 1210. (YS, 23) As Ruth Dunnell indicates, this annual tribute obligation "renewed the unsatisfactory situation that the Mongols found themselves in vis-à-vis the Jin in the 1160s." (Dunnell 2010, 36) Thus. after 30 years, the Mongols' situation had not changed significantly—but it would in the next decade.

With the successful Tatar campaign completed, Temüjin turned to deal with internal matters. The following incident reveals just how much Temüjin had matured since Dalan Baljut. When he attacked the Tatars, Temüjin's army was not at full strength, as the Jürkin Mongols, another group affiliated with the Borjigids, did not arrive at the arranged rendezvous point, even though Temüjin waited for them for six days. A few days prior to the campaign, the Borjigid Mongols held a *quriltai*. During the feast, Qorijin Khatun and Qu'urchin Khatun, the wives of the Jürkin leader Sacha Beki, became offended when one of Temüjin's men served a lady of lower standing before them. They beat the servant. Then, an incident occurred outside. Someone associated with the Jürkin attempted to steal a horse but was caught by Belgütei. He then got into an argument with Büri-Bökö, a wrestler of great renown among the Jürkin, over the man's guilt. In the scuffle, Büri-Bökö drew his sword and cut

Belgütei. Temüjin witnessed the events. The wounding of his stepbrother was too much. As they prohibited weapons during the feast (probably because of the heavy drinking), he grabbed a tree branch to avenge Belgütei. Belgütei told him the wound was minor and not worth rash actions, but Temüjin's anger got the better of him. The fight quickly escalated into a brawl throughout the feasting area. In the end, no one was seriously hurt, as they could only use what was readily available. After the Jürkin were soundly thrashed and Sacha Beki's wives briefly apprehended for their actions, the brawl ended. Although Temüjin displayed a temper and rash judgment, he focused on reconciliation. After a cooling-off period, Temüjin and Sacha Beki made amends, or so Temüjin thought.

The Jürkin did not take part in the Tatar campaign, but they did not sit idle. While Temüjin fought the Tatars, Sacha Beki, who had been among those who elevated Temüjin as khan, raided his camp, killing 10 of the men who had remained to guard it. After discovering the Jürkins' treachery, Temüjin attacked them, plundering them and capturing Sacha Beki and Taichu, the two leading Jürkin. He castigated them for their treachery and executed them. He permitted Belgütei to exact vengeance on Büri-Bökö, the famed wrestler, by defeating him and breaking his spine. With the Jürkins' betrayal, Temüjin understood that the only way for him to rule as khan was to eliminate competing lineages and develop loyalty among his own supporters rather than rely on the tenuous system of alliances between aristocratic lineages and cooperation that changed at the slightest hint of ill-fortune. Among the groups associated with the Jürkin were the Jalayirs. One of the Jalayirs, Ge'ün-u'a, presented his sons Muqali and Buqa to Temüjin and pledged them to his service. Other leaders did so as well. Like Jelme, these boys who began their service to Temüjin as servants did not remain in this position. Muqali rose to become one of Temüjin's leading generals, and arguably the second most powerful person in the Mongol Empire.

Shifts of power

Temüjin's actions with the Tatars and the Jürkin were only part of a larger shift of power in the steppes, all made with the tacit Jin support of the Kereit. This shift alarmed a number of other steppe polities. Jamuqa ended his service with Toghril and assembled a confederation to challenge the Kereit power. Taking the title of Gur Khan (universal ruler), Jamuqa's confederation of Naiman, Tatars, Jadaran, Tayichi'uds, and others encountered Toghril and Temüjin in 1201 at the Battle of Köyiten. Despite Jamuqa's forces engaging in weather magic to summon a storm, Toghril and Temüjin defeated the Gur-Khanid confederation. The storm backfired and had dire consequences for Jamuqa's side. Sensing defeat, Jamuqa plundered the camp of his allies and departed, with Toghril in pursuit. Defeated, Jamuqa once again became Toghril's *nökör*—a good general was a luxury one did not toss aside. Meanwhile, Temüjin pursued the Tayichi'ud Mongols to the Onan River, where he engaged them in battle. During the battle with the Tayichi'ud, Temüjin suffered a grievous arrow wound to his neck, which almost killed him. Despite the injury, he defeated the Tayichi'ud, exterminated their aristocracy, and incorporated those who did not escape into his own Borjigid Mongols. Tarqutai, however, who had taken Yisügei's people and then took Temüjin captive in his youth, fled.

Tarqutai did not escape unscathed, though. Some of his own subject people took him captive, thinking to surrender him to Temüjin. Tarqutai's sons attempted to rescue him, but the ringleader of the abductors, "Old man" Shirgü'etei held them off and threatened to kill Tarqutai. On their father's orders, Tarqutai's sons ceased their rescue attempts. He seemed to prefer to take his chances with Temüjin, believing that Temüjin would not kill him, or perhaps that Shirgü'etei would carry out his threat. Tarqutai viewed himself as a sort of father figure for Temüjin, remembering Temüjin's youthful captivity in a more noble manner, which may also indicate that Temüjin's captivity was less an enslavement and more of a foster son/educational moment:

> Saying that if I taught him
>   He would be likely to learn,
>   I kept teaching and instructing him just as if
>   He was a two or three-year-old new colt
>   I had been training.
>   Had I wanted him to die,
>   Would I not have been able to kill him?
> They say that at present
>   He is becoming thoughtful *in his actions*,
>   That his mind is clear. (SHM, §149)

Convinced that Temüjin would look upon him respectfully, Tarqutai convinced his sons to go away. Meanwhile, Old Man Shirgü'etei's sons, Alaq and Naya'a had second thoughts and became convinced that if they took Tarqutai to Temüjin, things would not go well for them. After all, they were part of a subordinate clan that had taken advantage of the Tayichi'ud's defeat to capture their leader. What would Temüjin do? Would he trust such men? Eventually, they convinced their father of the error of their way, released Tarqutai, and proceeded to Temüjin's camp. They then submitted to Temüjin and explained the recent events to him. Temüjin's response showed his maturity and his appreciation of the long view of events. Although he had a quick temper, Temüjin was not angry that Tarqutai was freed. He informed the men that they were correct in releasing Tarqutai, as he would have executed them for such an action—how could he trust men who turned on their master when circumstances became dire? As Naya'a showed the most intelligence and character in the incident, Temüjin showed him favor and eventually, Naya'a became one of the captains of his guard.

   The defeat of the Tayichi'ud continued to shower Temüjin with favor. Among those Temüjin gained was the family of Sorqan Shira, the very people who had taken pity on him and aided his escape years earlier, while Temüjin was a captive in the Tayichi'ud camp. He also acquired a man of no great importance among the Tayichi'ud. His name was Jirqo'adai. During the battle, he shot Temüjin's horse out from under him. It is likely that he is also the one who caused Temüjin's neck wound. Jirqo'adai was captured in the aftermath and boldly confessed that he was the one who shot the arrow that killed the horse.

Impressed by his boldness and forthright nature (not to mention his skill with a bow), Temüjin said, "A man who used to be an enemy, when it comes to his *former* killings and hostile actions 'conceals his person and hides his tongue'—he is afraid. As for this one, however, he does not hide his killings and hostile actions; he makes them known. He is a man to have as a companion." (SHM, §147) Temüjin then gave him a new name, Jebe, meaning arrow. Jebe proved his worth and loyalty on multiple occasions, becoming one of the most talented and innovative generals in the Mongol Empire, as well as in world history. Had this battle not occurred, or had Temüjin died from the wound, Jirqo'adai would have disappeared in the mists of history.

Temüjin recovered and then carried out his own campaign against the Tatars, neutralizing them permanently at the Battle of Dalan Nemürges near the Khalka River in eastern Mongolia. They executed most men, with only boys shorter than the axle of an ox cart being spared. Temüjin also acquired two wives, the sisters Yisüi and Yisügen. His victory over the Tatars in 1202 carried great significance, as it made him the dominant force in eastern Mongolia and theoretically extending Toghril's influence in that direction as well, even though the Kereit did not participate in the campaign. The warm relationship between Toghril and Temüjin faltered, however. Sources indicate that Toghril succumbed to the jealousies of his son, Senggüm, Jamuqa, who was now back in Toghril's service, as well as disparaging words from Temüjin's relatives: Altan, Daritai, and Quchar. These three "uncles" elevated Temüjin as khan after he separated from Jamuqa, but Temüjin deprived them of loot after they disobeyed orders and pillaged the Tatar camps in 1202, before victory had been secured. Senggüm's ire, however, began earlier in Western Mongolia.

In 1199, Toghril and Temüjin joined forces to attack the Naiman, a confederation of eight groups (Naiman means "eight" in Mongolian) in the region around the Altai Mountains. Initially, the two men were quite successful and even crossed the Altai Mountains in pursuit of Buyiruq Khan, one of the two Naiman khans. Toghril sought to impose his authority on the Naiman. After defeating Buyiruq Khan and plundering his camp, Toghril and Temüjin attempted to return across the mountains, but a Naiman commander Kökse'ü-sabraq intercepted them. The encounter occurred late in the day, near dusk; battle did not start due to nightfall. Undoubtedly unhappy about the return of his *anda*, Jamuqa convinced Toghril to move his camp in the middle of the night by persuading him that Temüjin plotted against Toghril in league with the Naiman.

The next morning, Temüjin and Kökse'ü-sabraq both learned that Toghril had abandoned the battlefield. Temüjin also discovered that Kökse'ü-sabraq did not view Temüjin as a sufficient threat, as the Naiman simply left him and went in pursuit of Toghril. Before long, Temüjin received messengers from Toghril requesting help against the Naiman attack. Temüjin dutifully sent troops who not only staved off the Naiman attack, but also rescued Toghril's son, Senggüm, from certain capture after an arrow grievously wounded his horse. Not long afterwards, Toghril and Temüjin crossed the Altai and returned to their home pastures in the Orkhon valley and Onan-Kerülen basin, respectively.

Marriages of convenience

The Secret History paints Toghril as a grateful, yet worried ruler. This was not the first time that Temüjin had aided him, much as Yisügei had, and Toghril viewed Temüjin as his potential heir. (SHM, §164) After the victory over the Tatars at Köyiten in 1202, Temüjin proposed that his son Jochi should marry Senggüm's daughter, Cha'ur, and that Temüjin's daughter Qojin should marry one of Toghril's relatives. Naturally, Senggüm liked neither idea, as he viewed Temüjin as an upstart angling for Senggüm's rightful throne. Although kinship ideally unified the leadership of a tribe, that Temüjin was a Mongol and Toghril a Kereit mattered less because of the fluid nature of tribal identity, as demonstrated when the Ambaghai, a Tayichi'ud became the khan instead of one of the Borjigid Qabul Khan's sons. Of course, they could arrange familial connections through strategic marriages.

Senggüm denounced the proposal, suggesting that a Kereit woman would be marrying beneath her station if she wed a Mongol, whereas if a Mongol woman married a Kereit, it elevated her to being a queen. He refused to consent to the marriage, disappointing Temüjin. Sensing an opportunity, Jamuqa, once again in Toghril's service after his defeat, also weighed in, along with Altan and Quchar. They all slandered Temüjin. Jamuqa continued to tell Senggüm and Toghril that Temüjin had plotted with the Naiman leader, Tayang Khan, against Toghril. Although Toghril no longer trusted Jamuqa, his efforts ingratiated him with Senggüm. Even if Toghril had his doubts about Jamuqa's words, the fear of Temüjin joining the Naiman must have lurked in the back of Toghril's mind as the Kereit khanate sat directly between the domains of the Naiman and the Mongols. If those two joined forces, they could surely crush Toghril.

Altan and Quchar, still resentful about Temüjin stripping them of their plunder for disobeying orders, also whispered words of treachery. Their issues with Temüjin went beyond the plunder, however. They felt ignored and diminished in standing, as Temüjin shared looted goods in which social status did not equate to a larger share. Whereas they had perhaps raised him as khan with a view of Temüjin being a malleable puppet, since then Temüjin's trials and travails had tempered him into a man of resolve, with a mind of his own. Furthermore, his life had demonstrated that he could not rely on the loyalty of relatives alone. His closest confidantes were his wife and mother, as well as friends such as Bo'orchu, but not his brothers or other male relatives. Some of these friends, his *nökörs* like Muqali and Jelme, had originated as slaves. They led Temüjin's troops and received honors, while his "uncles" received disrespect, or at least that is what they claimed. In their eyes, Temüjin did not respect them and the natural order of the social order. Thus, they promised to support the Kereit if they attacked Temüjin. With this vow, Senggüm finally convinced Toghril to eliminate Temüjin.

Toghril invited Temüjin to his camp, ostensibly to discuss the betrothal, but he plotted to kill the Mongol leader. Fortunately for Temüjin, fate intervened. Two Kereit grooms overheard the plan while taking care of the horses, and they alerted Temüjin of the Kereit plot. While he was skeptical at first, he eventually discovered they spoke the truth and he did not attend the "betrothal." After this attempt to lure Temüjin into a trap failed, the Kereit and Mongols met in battle at Qalqajit Sands in 1203. Initially, the Kereit defeated the Mongols. Unlike in his first battle against Jamuqa at Dalan Baljut, Temüjin's forces were not routed. Instead, they regrouped at Lake Baljuna, a predesignated rendezvous point. There, they rested and then counter-attacked days later while the Kereit were still enjoying their initial victory. Jamuqa, Senggüm, and Toghril all escaped through different routes. Senggüm fled into Xi Xia, while Jamuqa eventually joined the Naiman. Toghril also fled west, but a Naiman scout failed to recognize the Kereit Khan and killed him. Despite his death, Toghril's skull became an object of veneration in the tent of Gürbesü, where the Naiman Khatun, or queen, attempted to tap into any spiritual power the deceased khan might offer. The *Yuanshi*, a Chinese chronicle of the record of the Mongol Empire, omits the Lake Baljuna event and indicates that Temüjin defeated the Kereit in the first battle. I suspect they did this to show that Temüjin had never been defeated, just as the *Yuanshi* improbably has Temüjin defeating Jamuqa at Dalan Baljut. Still, the *Yuanshi* also includes a litany of offenses that Toghril committed against Temüjin, despite the latter's unfaltering loyalty to the Kereit khan. Toghril's betrayal is contrasted with Yisügei's and Temüjin's efforts in assisting Toghril to maintain his throne, even when Toghril lost it on more than one occasion, and often because he proved perfidious and jealous, demonstrating that Temüjin had more regal characteristics. (YS, 12, 13, 19)

Temüjin's respite at Lake Baljuna was significant on many levels. On one hand, it allowed his army to regroup and his son, Ögödei, to recover from a neck wound. While his initial defeat was not a route, his army dispersed with an intent to meet at Lake Baljuna. Boroqul, Temüjin's foster brother, brought the severely wounded Ögödei with him to the Lake Baljuna, after the rest of the army had already arrived. Additionally, a number of individuals drank the muddy waters of Lake Baljuna and took an oath of allegiance to Temüjin in this moment of seeming defeat. What is notable is that none of the Baljuntu, as they became known, were Mongols. While a few originated from the steppes, others were Muslims from Central Asia, as well as a couple of Khitans from the Jin Empire. These individuals would later play important roles in a wide range of capacities in the development of the Mongol Empire, but it is notable that the list did not include relatives. The absence of blood relatives demonstrated Temujin's emphasis on personal loyalty over kinship ties.

A turning point

The victory over the Kereit was a major turning point for Temüjin, not only in military terms, but also in status. The victory also legitimized him. The Secret Historian records that victorious Temüjin remembered the two grooms who informed him of Toghril's treachery, but also that he now gained Toghril's kingdom. Temüjin said, "Because of the vital service performed by Badai and Kisiliq, and under the protection of Eternal Heaven, I crushed the Kereyit people and, indeed, gained the high throne. In the future, the offspring of *my* offspring who will occupy *this* throne of mine must successively remember those *two* who performed such service!" (SHM, §187) Clearly, being the khan of the Kereit was more significant than being the khan of the Borjigid Mongols. Part of the Kereit's prestige was the location of the Kereit Khanate in Central Mongolia. Controlling the steppes watered by the Tula, Selenge, and Orkhon rivers that emptied into Lake Baikal, the Kereit possessed excellent pastures. Additionally, the Orkhon river valley had an allure to it. For centuries, possession of it conveyed legitimacy and authority to those who occupied it. During the era of the Xiongnu (200 BCE-202 CE) their empire centered on it. The Turks (552-743) also based their rule in the region. The Uighurs (744-840) even built a permanent capital city called Qarabalghasun there. The Mongols eventually followed suit, although it would be several decades before they built Qaraqorum, the capital of the Mongol Empire. In the meantime, Temüjin maintained his primary camp in his traditional home of the Onan-Kerulen basin.

With the defeat of the Kereit, the Mongols now dominated approximately half of Mongolia. Other tribes existed, but these were minor compared to the Mongols and the Naiman. Like the Kereit, the Naiman could not be compared with the Mongols. Just as the Kereit elite snubbed their noses at the Mongols in terms of culture and sophistication, so did the Naiman. As a tribal confederation occupying much of western Mongolia and the regions around the Altai Mountains in modern Kazakhstan and Xinjiang, the Naiman were considerably more sophisticated, including possessing a degree of literacy and embracing a world religion (Nestorian Christianity like the Kereit) that gave them access to larger world in terms of trade, cultural, and political relations. It did not, however, improve their attitude. They viewed the Mongols as crude and socially unacceptable. When the Naiman khan, Tayang Khan, proposed to take the Mongols captive, Gürbesü Khatun, Tayang's mother, said, "What could we do with them? The Mongol people have *always* smelt bad and worn grimy clothes. They live apart, and far away. Let them stay *there*. But we might perhaps have their fine daughters- and daughters-in-law brought here and, making them wash their hands, perhaps just let them milk our cows and sheep." (SHM, §189) Clearly, Gürbesü had little regard for the status of the Mongols.

Not fearing the Mongols' lack of hygiene, the Naiman sought to seize the former Kereit pastures from Mongol control and Tayang Khan proposed they attack the Mongols. Kökese'ü-sabraq, the Naiman general who had some experience fighting the Mongols, cautioned against this, but was ignored. Determined to bring the upstart Mongols to heel, Tayang Khan and the Naiman moved east. Learning of the Naiman's advance, Temüjin led his own army to meet them in Central Mongolia. The two armies clashed at Chakirma'ut in 1204, with the Mongols emerging victorious, despite the Naiman holding the high ground.

The victory was greater than simply defeating the Naiman. With the Kereit's defeat, all those who had opposed Temüjin rallied to Tayang Khan's side. Jamuqa was there, advising him, as were the Merkit. Despite the crushing defeat (quite literally as they forced many retreating Naiman off a cliff where they fell and piled up like logs), Jamuqa, ever the survivor, escaped. Those Mongols who followed him and continued to resist Temüjin's rule submitted after the battle. Yet, Jamuqa was not the only *anda* who was present among the Naiman; Jaqa Gambu and several of the Kereit were also there. Jaqa Gambu had fallen out with his brother, joining the Naiman before the Battle of Qalqajit Sands in 1203.

After the battle, Temüjin pardoned Jaqa Gambu and gave him great honor. Furthermore, he and Temüjin became even closer. If Senggüm had still been present, he would have been livid with his uncle. As Senggüm vehemently opposed the marriage of Cha'ur to Jochi in 1203, undoubtedly his disappointment would have escalated had he learned that not just one Kereit princess was to marry a Mongol, but three. Cha'ur was not involved. Curiously, she disappeared from history. Jochi, however, did not languish in his tent, lamenting his lost love. Instead, he married Jaqa Gambu's daughter Bektütmish, while his younger brother (Temüjin's youngest son), Tolui married her sister Sorqoqtani. Meanwhile,

Temüjin married Ibaqa, Jaqa Gambu's third daughter, oddly making him the brother-in-law of his sons. Despite the conflict, Jaqa Gambu and Temüjin remained on good terms, although now Jaqa Gambu was below Temüjin in status.

Although the Mongols did not fully secure Mongolia until 1208 at the Irtysh River—where Temüjin defeated the Naiman and Merkit, who had joined the Naiman prince Güchülüg—Temüjin became the ruler of Mongolia with his victory at Chakirma'ut in 1204. Unknown to the world, it is nevertheless one of the most important battles in world history. Here the Mongols demonstrated that their mode of warfare surpassed the traditional steppe warfare. Since the time of the Scythians, nomadic horse-archers had been the most dominant warriors on the battlefields of Eurasia. During Temüjin's rise to power, all his opponents had all been nomads. Thus he had to find novel ways of defeating the tactics that both sides knew intimately. Temüjin's new tactics, which included innovative formations and the ability of his units to transition from one formation to the next, changed the status quo of steppe warfare. Using deception such as lighting more campfires to disguise his numbers and releasing horses in Naiman territory in a weakened condition, Temüjin fed the Naiman false intelligence. With his new formations, Temüjin's troops moved seamlessly from marching formations to battle array, hemming the Naiman in, so that they could not deploy their superior numbers. Then the Mongols relentlessly showered the compacted mass of Naiman troops with arrows, waiting for the Naiman to break. Naiman efforts to penetrate the Mongols' lines failed due to the discipline of the Mongols and the fact that any forward movement from the Naiman allowed the Mongols to strike them from the rear. From this point onward, no other nomadic forces successfully opposed the Mongols, although nomads remained a formidable challenge.

With the Naiman defeated and the Mongols as the paramount military force in the steppes, Temüjin could now rest and consolidate his newly won empire and state. In the process of his life, he had gone from an ostracized child at the mercy of others to the most powerful person on the steppes. Temüjin had become Chinggis Khan.

4. Creation of the Yeke Monggol Ulus

With the defeat of the Naiman, the Mongols were the sole major power within Mongolia, although Temüjin continued mop-up operations against those who escaped defeat at Chakirma'ut, which included the Naiman prince Güchülüg, some Merkit leaders, and the wily Jamuqa. As the Mongol armies began operations to finish any further opposition, the Mongols also held a *quriltai* at the headwaters of the Onan River, formally enthroning Temüjin as Chinggis Khan, a title meaning firm or fierce leader, in 1206. Chinggis Khan also began organizing his newly won empire at this time.

The *quriltai* that selected Temüjin as Chinggis Khan had no other candidates since they had been eliminated through the unification of Mongolia, a process that was not planned but one that happened in fits and starts. The *quriltai* and events afterwards did more than ceremoniously recognize Temüjin as the ruler of the Mongolian steppes. In this process, Chinggis Khan started a social revolution that fundamentally altered society, stripping away old identities in order to form the *Yeke Monggol Ulus*, or Great Mongol Nation. The idea was that there would be no more Kereit or Naiman, etc., but everyone would be Mongol. Chinggis Khan laid the foundations for a state while he was still Temüjin. Having realized that the Jürkin could not be trusted and would always vie for the leadership of the Mongols, he eradicated their leading figures. Subsequently, he did this for most tribes that he fought. The Kereit were the exception, but only because of his close relationship with Jaqa Gambu. There can be little doubt of what would have happened to Toghril and Senggüm had they not escaped. To rule this massive new entity and through the process of unification, Chinggis Khan had destroyed the old aristocratic lineages and established a single royal family, the *altan urugh* or Golden Family, based on one's blood relationship to him. Finally, he ended the patron/*nökör* institution, which did not disappear overnight. Rather, it evolved into a new entity.

Replacing the *nökör* was the *noyan*. Although the term eventually became the equivalent of "lord," it originally meant commander and was used at all organizational levels such as *arban-u noyan* (commander of 10) or *minggan-u noyan* (commander of 1000). Rather than the *nökör* who owed service to an individual in return for various forms of compensation, but also retained the ability to end his service, the *noyan* owed his service and position directly to the position of the khan—not to an individual but to the institution. Furthermore, the *noyan* could be replaced at the discretion of the khan. Although a khan could dismiss a *nökör*, that individual could then seek service elsewhere. The *noyan* could not, as there were no other options. Indeed, Chinggis Khan specifically stated that if one could not perform his duties adequately, then he should not serve in that capacity (JT, 201). Who would replace him? The next man in his unit. Each man in a squad of 10 should be prepared to lead if necessary. It was an idea akin to the Napoleonic practice of every man carrying a marshal's baton in his knapsack.

Besides the *noyans*, others also received privileges from Chinggis Khan for services rendered to him during his rise to power. This included the family of Sorqan Shira who had aided him while he was a prisoner of the Tayichi'ud, as well as the two Kereit grooms, Badai and Kisiliq, who warned him of Toghril and Senggüm's treachery. The privileges these individuals received ranged from certain tax exemptions, immunity from punishment for up to nine crimes, as well as being designated freemen who could wear a quiver (slaves were not allowed to carry bows and arrows). While Chinggis Khan's commanders and these other esteemed figures ranged from members of the old aristocracy to former servants such as Muqali and Jelme, their status within Chinggis Khan's new *Yeke Monggol Ulus* was based on their merit. Birthright mattered little in the eyes of Chinggis Khan. Aside from the ruling lineage of the *Altan Urugh*, the rest of society was to be governed through a meritocracy. Yet this idea was fleeting. After the death of Chinggis Khan, the position of *noyan* became increasingly hereditary due to Chinggis Khan's own generosity of rewarding not only individuals, but their offspring as well. While it was still possible to advance through merit, a true meritocracy faded away. The older noyan lineages gradually transformed into a new aristocracy, particularly when they married a Chinggisid princess.

Chinggis Khan awarded 95 commanders *minggans*. The assignment of *minggans* or units of a thousand allowed Chinggis Khan to reward his supporters and also transform society into a meritocracy as the commanders came from all social levels. While Chinggis Khan's immediate family members were not included, his sons-in-law were. Through marriage, Chinggis Khan's daughters connected him to other important figures and families, reinforcing their relationship. The daughters were not passive actors, while they served as rewards to someone fortunate enough to marry one. The sons-in-law, known as *güregen*, were permitted to be commanders of multiple *minggans*, to show respect but also to build a cadre of men with troops tied directly to Chinggis Khan through his daughters. His eldest daughter, Qojin, married Butu of the Ikires, who commanded two *minggans* or his own Ikires warriors. Checheyigen, the second daughter, would marry the son of Quduqa Beki, the leader of the Oirat, a tribe in the forests of Siberia who submitted to Jochi in 1207. The son's name remains uncertain. The third daughter, Alaqa, married into the Önggüds. Their leader, Alaqush Digit Quri, had warned Temüjin of the Naiman's intent to attack. For his service, the Önggüd were not dispersed and Alaqush and his sons commanded five *minggans* of their own troops. Tümelün, the fourth daughter, married into the Önggirad, the tribe of her mother, maintaining that vital connection. Her husband, Chigu, commanded three to five *minggans*. The youngest daughter, Al Altan, would marry Barchuk, the Idiqut or ruler of the Uighurs, who submitted to Chinggis Khan in 1209. Like the Oirat, the Uighurs were outside the steppes, but the marriage bound the Uighurs to Chinggis Khan and it was an important incentive for the Idiqut to submit to Chinggis Khan, as he had been a vassal of Qara Khitai. Comprising their own troops (not mixed with the defeated) indicates that Chinggis Khan viewed them with trust and they had submitted in good faith. The daughters, however, were not simply pawns. In all instances, they also served as viceroys on Chinggis Khan's behalf, thus extending his authority. While they did not rule directly, they served as his eyes and ears, while receiving instructions from him. (Broadbridge, 107-129)

Other commanders were companions of Chinggis Khan, his former *nökör*, or former servants, who proved their worth and trust. Some, like Jebe, had even started as enemies. Appreciating their loyalty, Chinggis Khan promoted them to leading positions. To Temüjin, loyalty was the most important trait in a person. If they proved loyal, there was no limit to their use or importance in his eyes. Jebe, who gave himself up only when all was lost, is an example of this. Naya'a is another. He wisely did not hand over Tarqutai to Chinggis Khan, as that would have been an act of betrayal and he most likely would have been executed. A similar circumstance arose after the Battle of Chakirma'ut. Jamuqa once again escaped the battle, but after months of living on the run as a bandit, his men bound him and turned him over to Chinggis Khan. To their surprise, Temüjin executed Jamuqa's comrades, as they had proven that they could not be trusted, particularly during bad times. He also executed Jamuqa, although if *The Secret History of the Mongols* is to be believed, Chinggis Khan had a hard time deciding because of his fondness for Jamuqa. In the end, Jamuqa had to convince Chinggis Khan that they must execute him. (SHM, §200-201) This scenario is difficult to believe and is most likely a hagiography demonstrating Chinggis Khan's clemency and his own loyalty to his *anda*. Other than the pre-Dalan Baljut era, there had been little occasion for Chinggis Khan and Jamuqa to bond. Aside from the fact that Jamuqa had been the only person to defeat Chinggis Khan decisively and thus demonstrated some tactical ability, there is little reason to think that Chinggis Khan needed him.

The importance of loyalty

Temüjin's emphasis on loyalty may also be tied to the eradication of the traditional patron/*nökör* relationship. Previously, the relationship had been strictly between the patron and his bondsman: a patron could dismiss *nökörs* he found no longer useful, while a *nökör* could leave when he felt the situation was no longer tenable. This is quite clear during Chinggis Khan's childhood, after his father's death. While I am dubious that Yisügei's family was completely abandoned, a number of Yisügei's *nökörs* left and found service among the Tayichi'ud or elsewhere. The effort was to secure loyalty that otherwise might be ephemeral and lasted only as long as a particular ruler sat on the throne. Under the new system, commanders could only pledge themselves to a single individual, Chinggis Khan and, by extension, his family. No other fountains of authority flowed, no other power existed. To not serve Chinggis Khan meant one did not dwell in the *Yeke Monggol Ulus*. Still, this loyalty was not meant to be blind. He expected his *noyans* to advise him, particularly his inner circle, who could tell him when he was mistaken or making a poor decision. While Chinggis Khan appreciated loyalty, he did not value "yes" men, as their only loyalty was truly to themselves.

Chinggis Khan achieved this singular loyalty by eliminating other lineages of the tribal aristocracy through several methods. Although the primary method of elimination was through executions, he also suborned other lineages to the *Altan urugh* by marriage with his daughters. Marriage with the male Chinggis descendants also secured loyalty. For instance, with the Kereit, Jaqa Gambu was spared despite fighting Chinggis Khan at the Qalqajit Sands, but his daughters were then married to Chinggis Khan as well as his sons Tolui and Jochi. While most of the Tatar leadership was eliminated, Chinggis Khan married two Tatar women, Yisüi and Yisülen, as previously mentioned. Then in 1205, the Merkit were once again defeated. While most fled westward into modern Kazakhstan, one group remained, led by Dayir-usun. He, the Merkit leader of the Qo'as Merkit (one of the three Merkit groups) submitted to Chinggis Khan and married his daughter Qulan to the Mongol leader. Another woman taken from the spoils of the Merkit defeat also became an important wife in the *Yeke Monggol Ulus*. This woman, named Töregene, had been the wife of Qudu, a Merkit prince. While Qudu fled to the Irtysh River, Chinggis Khan captured her and gave her to his son, Ögödei, as a wife. She is even more remarkable as she was a Naiman; her marriage to Qudu helped form an alliance and one reason the Merkit cooperated with the Naiman frequently. These women were not simply concubines for the amusement of their husbands—if they had been, they would not have become wives. By marrying them (whether by choice), the women took on a new status. They would be expected to run their own households. By household, I don't mean simply their husband's ger (each wife had her own), but also the camp and all personnel associated with it. Wives often managed camps with hundreds of people, ranging from servants, administrative staff, guards, and a host of others. The wives of Chinggis Khan could expect even more. Chinggis Khan usually campaigned with one of his wives, who then managed his camp. As a result, the wives wielded considerable power. Also, their children became Mongol princes. With their new status and offspring, their old identity faded and only the Mongol one remained.

Those who married into Chinggis Khan's family benefitted as well, but they were never on the same level. As Dayir-usun formally submitted and married Qulan to Chinggis Khan, the Mongol leader spared the captured Merkits and kept them intact instead of distributing them among the *minggans*. Eventually, they rose in rebellion and were squashed. He then distributed the remaining Merkit among the existing regiments. Dayir-usun is notably not found among the 95 commanders, whereas Alaqush Digit Quri of the Önggüd, whose son married Alaqa, one of Chinggis Khan's daughters, is on the rolls as a commander, albeit his five *minggans* are his own Önggüd troop. This contrast is interesting as it shows that although Qulan married Chinggis Khan, her father could not maintain his own status as a leader due to the Merkit rebellion. Chinggis Khan, however, allowed Alaqush Digit Quri to keep his people intact. Of course, this was due not only to the marriage to Alaqa, but also because he warned Chinggis Khan of the Naiman's plans in 1204. Nonetheless, it is clear that status was conveyed through the favor of the khan, but he could also withdraw it as with Dayir-usun. An interesting comparison that fits somewhere between the status of son-in-law and father-in-law of Chinggis Khan was Jürchedei. He led the Uru'ut, a tribe or clan of the Mongols who fought alongside Chinggis Khan in many battles and played a key role at Qalqajit Sands and Chakirma'ut. The Uru'ut were viewed as elite troops not only among the Mongols, but by the Kereit and Naiman as well. During the 1206 *quriltai*, Chinggis Khan awarded Jürchedei's service by giving him Ibaqa, Chinggis Khan's Kereit wife. This does not appear to be Chinggis Khan simply pawning off an unwanted wife, but an award of great honor as she maintained her royal status. Curiously, one service Jürchedei rendered for Chinggis Khan included killing Ibaqa's father Jaqa Gambu after the latter turned against Chinggis Khan between 1204 and 1206. As the details are vague, we do not know what exactly transpired between Chinggis Khan and his father-in-law.

Decimal-based units

However, the key to this transition from confederation to state was not merely the elimination of rivals or of the *nökör* system, or the establishment of the *noyans*, but the switch to a decimal system of military units of tens, hundreds, and thousands. This last unit, known as a *minggan*, became the standard unit of organization not only for the military but also for all of society. Eventually, another unit known as the *tümen* , or ten thousand, was also used. The reliance on decimal-based units was not Chinggis Khan's innovation, but it had a long, albeit irregular, history in Inner Asia, dating back to the Xiongnu or Huns (circa 200 BCE-200 CE). In all likelihood, Chinggis Khan adopted it from the Kereit. He permitted those who had been loyal or submitted without resistance (such as the Önggüd and Onggirad) to remain together as coherent groups but divided into units of a thousand. By contrast, other defeated groups, such as the Naiman and Tayichi'ud, were sprinkled among the *minggans* of loyal groups or distributed into *minggans* cobbled together from diverse groups—both defeated and allies. At the *quriltai*, these regiments were then divvied up among Temüjin's commanders. All were to be considered Mongols, whether they were originally Onggirad, Kereit, or Merkit. Also of great significance was that each *minggan's noyan* or commander was in charge not only of the military regiment, but also the soldier's households, thus structuring society to support the military units.

The final tool through which Chinggis Khan forged the bonds of loyalty was through the creation of the *keshig*, or bodyguard. Shortly before the Battle of Chakirma'ut, Chinggis Khan created a bodyguard comprising 80-night guards and 70-day guards, plus 1000 men who accompanied Temüjin into battle. After the creation of the *Yeke Monggol Ulus*, the bodyguard, or *keshig*, increased to 10,000 men with 8000-day guards, 1000 night guards, and 1000 quiver bearers, whose role remains murky. Why the massive increase? After all, it did not mean that 10,000 men followed Chinggis Khan at all times in dark suits and sunglasses, serving as a human wall around him. Rather, they had shifts and other duties such as cooking, as well as tending to the khan's herds and flocks. The *keshig* formed the household staff of the ruler in all meanings of the term. In battle, still, only 1,000 accompanied Chinggis Khan. The others remained at the camp to help guard it. Furthermore, each wife had a camp. By 1206, when Chinggis Khan formally took the throne, he had at least six wives: Börte, Yisui, Yisülen, Ibaqa, Gürbesü, and Qulan. The expansion of his authority, along with the growing number of his wives, necessitated the enlargement of the *keshig*. Not only was more manpower required to protect Chinggis

Khan's own person, but also his wives, just as American secret service agents protect not only the current American President and his family, but they continue to safeguard past presidents as well, but on a smaller scale.

So who comprised the *keshig*? The solution was to fill it with the sons of his commanders, not just the high-ranking ones, but even the commanders of *jaghuns* (100) and *arbans*, as well as commoners of talent. The young men served both as guards, household staff, but also as hostages. It was an old practice in which sons stayed in the camp (which may have been Temüjin's experience with the Tayichi'ud) to not only ensure loyalty, but also to train. For Chinggis Khan and later Mongol rulers, these hostages were not simply to ensure good behavior from distant vassals, but also to train the sons and bind them to the *Yeke Monggol Ulus*, so that if a ruler needed to be replaced, they had a suitable substitute waiting in the wings. As a result, the *keshig* was not all Mongols or even nomads. Additionally, it is notable that most of the major commanders and governors after the Chinggis Khan's companions died, emerged from the *keshig*.

With a new state, Chinggis Khan also needed a more defined legal system. It was based on law and tradition, known as *yasa* and *yosun*, respectively. While *yosun*, or tradition, referred to the customs of the Mongols, which were commonplace for most of the nomads of Mongolia, the *yasa* referred to the decrees and laws that Chinggis Khan made. Although the sources refer to *yasa* and *yosun*, in many instances the difference also became blurred. This, in part, was because a complete document did not exist or was largely reserved for the Mongols, not for subjects or even their bureaucratic servants. Chinggis Khan assigned his foster-brother, Shiqi Qutuqu, to record his decrees and serve as the high judge (*yeke jarquchi*) of the empire. Thus, non-Mongols had an incomplete sense of the law. This may seem odd from a modern perspective, but one can also argue that the average American citizens lack a complete understanding of the U. S. Constitution. The situation is the same in most countries. We learn the basics (hopefully not from breaking the law), but few read and study it thoroughly. More importantly, in the case of the Mongol Empire, the initial *Yasa* was designed for ruling an empire of nomads. As the empire expanded, the *Yasa* metamorphosed to suit the needs of new rulers. Indeed, there also appears to have been some debate during the reign of Ögödei (r. 1229-1241) about how the *Yasa* should be applied—the Mongols or the entire empire (May 2018, 102-103). To be sure, the *Yasa* always trumped all other legal practices, but the Mongols generally allowed pre-existing practices to continue, as long as they did not interfere with Mongol priorities.

5. Campaigns of Chinggis Khan (1205-1227)

It is difficult to imagine that much of the geographic territory of the People's Republic of China results from the Mongol and Qing Empires. In the 13th century, half a dozen kingdoms existed within the modern borders. Only three could be considered "Chinese" in terms of governing style and only one in terms of dynastic ethnicity. The Jin Empire (1125-1234) was of Manchurian origin, covering that region and north China, extending west to the Ordos Loop (where the Huanghe, or Yellow River, forms an open rectangle). While the ruling elite were Jurchen (Manchurian), the rest of the population included the Han Chinese, but also Khitans, a Mongolic people who previously ruled north China and much of Mongolia and Manchuria as the Liao Empire (906-1125). As mentioned previously, Jin control extended into Inner Mongolia (the steppe region south of the Gobi but north of the Yin Shan mountains), although direct rule fluctuated in any year. On the Jin's western border rested the kingdom of Xi Xia (1038-1227), ruled by the Tangut, a Tibetan people, although the region also had a sizeable Han and Turkic population. The modern provinces of Ningxia, Gansu, and parts of Shaanxi, Xinjiang, and Inner Mongolia comprised its territory. That it straddled key parts of the Silk Road gave it considerable economic importance. Militarily, it was not equal to the Jin Empire, and often paid the latter tribute. To the south resided the Song, or rather Southern Song Empire (960-1279,) as the Liao Empire took the Song's northern territories, which the Jin then occupied. While the Jin Empire and Xi Xia used Chinese institutions, the Song Empire was a true Chinese Empire ruled by ethnic Chinese rulers. While it paled compared to the Jin militarily, the Song's economic might permitted it to resist further Jin encroachment, even as the Song dynasty dreamed of restoring its former northern territories. The regions of Tibet and most of Xinjiang were not part of any Chinese kingdom, nor was the province of Yunnan. These regions had their own kingdoms or were affiliated with other empires, such as Qara Khitai, which will be discussed later.

Despite unifying Mongolia, Chinggis Khan did not rest on his laurels. Before long, the Mongol armies were once again on the move. He sent armies in pursuit of those leaders who had fled Mongolia. Armies marched west in pursuit of the Naiman and Merkit. Meanwhile, his son Jochi led armies into Siberia to bring the *Hoyin-Irgen*, or Forest peoples (which included the Oirat and Kyrgyz), into the Mongol realm, while also securing access to the fur trade as well as grain and gold from the Yenisei River basin. Meanwhile, the Kereit prince Senggüm fled to Xi Xia after Chinggis Khan defeated the Kereit in 1203. Thus, an army searched for Senggüm while raiding Xi Xia in 1205. Although the Tangut rulers of Xi Xia evicted Senggüm due to his own pillaging, Chinggis Khan became determined to ensure that outside powers could not meddle in the affairs of Mongolia. He well knew the possibility of this happening and we must remember his rise to power occurred through the interference of a non-nomadic power, the Jin. The defeat of the Tatars by Temüjin, Toghril, and a Jin army dramatically shifted the balance of the power in eastern Mongolia, thus allowing the rise of Chinggis Khan.

The invasion of Xi Xia 1205 marked Chinggis Khan's first war against a sedentary power. While this invasion has sometimes been viewed as a practice run for an invasion of the Jin Empire, this is not accurate, and projects later events back to this moment. Nonetheless, the invasion of Xi Xia played an important part in transforming the *Yeke Monggol Ulus* from a steppe polity into a true empire. Even though Senggüm was no longer in Xi Xia, Chinggis Khan still had valid reasons to invade—securing Mongolia from troublesome neighbors who often meddled in steppe affairs. That Senggüm initially took refuge there demonstrated that Xi Xia could still serve as a base or refuge for other nomadic leaders who opposed Chinggis Khan or grew dissatisfied with his rule. Indeed,

Xi Xia had long served as a haven for deposed steppe leaders, who often staged their comeback from there. It was in Chinggis Khan's interest to eliminate this possibility. An invasion also gave him an opportunity to raid, so he could plunder goods for his supporters while also giving his newly created army something to do—if left to its own devices, there was still an opportunity for old rivalries to spawn again. Invading was, in a sense, a team-building exercise—nothing builds camaraderie like going some place where other people will try to kill you as they simply see you as an invader and not as Kereit, Naiman, Mongol, or Merkit. While raids began in 1205 in search of Senggüm, they continued into 1206. Recognizing the futility in engaging the Mongols in combat, the Tangut (the ruling group in Xi Xia) simply sat behind their fortifications. This passive response to invasion, however, did not sit well with some, leading to a coup that brought Li Anquan (1206-1211) to the throne. Chinggis Khan did not lead the initial raid, but one of his new commanders, a Khitan named Yelü Ahai, who had previously been Jin Empire's envoy to Toghril's court. While he met Chinggis Khan in the 1190s at Toghril's court, it is possible that Yelü Ahai and his brother, Yelü Tuha, met Temüjin when he was in the Jin Empire. Regardless, the two Khitans were present with Temüjin at Lake Baljuna and the Battle of Qalqajit Sands. At the very least, these two had joined Temüjin by 1203.

Mongol raids continued until spring 1208, with Chinggis Khan attacking the frontier city of Wuluhai in 1207. That year, his armies also trounced the Naiman-Merkit coalition that Güchülüg had assembled at the Irtysh River. Güchülüg escaped, but they nullified any potential threat from the Güchülüg, at least temporarily, allowing Chinggis Khan to focus his attention on Xi Xia. It is uncertain why he ceased raiding and turned to conquest, although he may have heard of Li Anquan's efforts to form an alliance with the Jin Empire against the Mongols in 1208. The Jin rebuffed these efforts, with the Jin Emperor saying, "It is to our advantage when our enemies attack one another. Wherein lies the danger to us?" (Dunnell 1994, 207)

Despite the Jin's lack of interest, the proposed alliance had the potential to undermine everything Chinggis Khan had accomplished. From that perspective, he had the incentive to eliminate Xi Xia as a threat as quickly as possible. After capturing Wulahai, a fortress city on the Huanghe River, he marched towards the capital city, Zhongxing. After defeating an army that sought to halt the Mongol invasion, the Mongols settled down to besiege the city. The Mongols lacked experience in siege warfare and their endeavors were crude, but effective. Besides blockading the city, the Mongols became more creative as they lacked proper siege engines. They diverted a river to flood the city and in the process flooded their own camp as well. Their determination (and perhaps recklessness) convinced Li Anquan to submit to Chinggis Khan. In 1209, the Mongols departed Xi Xia with their plunder and tribute comprising silks, silver, camels, hunting falcons, and also Chaqa, a Tangut princess to be a new wife for Chinggis Khan—his sixth of seven in total. Although he also had many concubines, when Chinggis Khan took a new wife, it was political strategy, formalizing a submission with a marriage alliance. The Tangut also promised to supply troops when requested. In return, the Mongols departed and did not occupy Xi Xia.

Forays into the Jin Empire

Unlike Xi Xia, the Jin Empire (1125-1234) proved to be a tougher nut to crack, as it was arguably the most powerful state in the world. Initially, it does not appear that Chinggis Khan sought war with the Jin Empire, but probably recognized that they would meddle in his affairs. He also had not forgotten Ambaghai Khan's execution and longed to avenge Mongol honor. It was standing practice among the Jin (and previous dynasties) to prevent the unification of the steppe tribes. Chinggis Khan experienced this as the Jin and Tatars broke the first Mongol Khanate in the 12th century, and then Chinggis

Khan himself took part in a Jin-inspired effort to break the Tatars who had then grown too powerful. The Jin had carefully constructed a balancing act to keep the nomads in turmoil. While this could lead to raids, as there was no single power in the steppes, these forays were relatively minor (for the empire, not the victims) compared to what a single steppe ruler could do with the combined military power of all tribes.

That Chinggis Khan had unified the steppe demonstrated not only his own abilities, but also the Jin's longstanding neglect of steppe affairs. A factor in this turn of events was that the *jüyin*, the various tribes and other groups who guarded the frontiers of the Jin Empire, rebelled against the Jin at the beginning of the 13th century. This rebellion allowed the Önggüd, who dwelled in what is now Inner Mongolia, People's Republic of China, to join Chinggis Khan. A war with the Chinese Song Empire to the south of the Jin Empire also diverted the Jin's attention from 1206 to 1208. While the Jin handled these issues, it gave Chinggis Khan time to strengthen his position because the Jin failed to address all the reasons that led to the *jüyin* rebellion.

Still, Chinggis Khan surely realized it was only a matter of time before the Jin would take action against him, whether directly or perhaps finding Güchülüg or another candidate among the defeated steppe leaders. Yet this does not mean that war was inevitable, although the Jin construction of the Wusha fortress near the border in 1210 may have provoked some skirmishing between the Mongols and the Jin. The *Yuan shi* indicates that the construction of the fortress would be the first phase of a campaign against the Mongols. (YS, 23) The Mongols, however, pre-empted any Jin action. A key and often under-appreciated element in the tensions between the Mongols and the Jin was that the Jin also acquired a new ruler. Emperor Jing (also called Zhangzong) had been in power long enough that Chinggis Khan respected him, even if he did not like him. Chinggis Khan knew that conflict with Emperor Jing was not a task lightly taken, particularly as he had a ruthless reputation. (YS, 22) When an emissary came from the Jin Empire to collect tribute, indicating that Chinggis Khan was still a hypothetical vassal of the Jin, as indicated by his *jaut quri* title, he also learned that a new emperor, Yunji, the former Prince of Wei, sat on the Jin throne. Chinggis Khan knew him personally, and had little respect for him. Indeed, when Yunji had been an emissary and collected tribute, Chinggis Khan despised him. Once the new emissary informed Chinggis Khan that Yunji became the new emperor with the title of Weishao Wang, he viewed his relationship in a new light. Prior to this point, Chinggis Khan had been a vassal of the Jin, but with the death of the previous emperor Jing (r. 1189-1208), who also ruled during the Tatar campaign, Temüjin viewed those agreements as null and void. Indeed, when informed of the new emperor by the Jin envoy, Chinggis Khan spat in the direction of the Jin Empire and rode away without showing obeisance or presenting tribute. (YS, 23) The fact that Chinggis Khan showed disrespect and refused to deliver tribute to Jin officials demanded retaliation as well. He undoubtedly realized this. Naturally, Emperor Yunji (r.1208-1213) became angry when informed of this insubordination, but rather than invade the steppes, he preferred to wait until the next scheduled tribute payment. Then, or so he plotted, he would destroy Chinggis Khan. The Mongol leader, however, had no plans to resume tribute payments. Thus, in 1211, the Chinggis Khan began the invasion, leaving his younger brother Temüge in Mongolia as his regent.

The invasion began in April 1211, after the Mongols' horses had recovered from the winter. Before departing from the Kerulen River, Chinggis Khan ascended a mountain and prayed to Köke Möngke Tengri, the Blue Eternal Sky, and chief god of the steppe people. He asked for Heaven's (Tengri's) favor to avenge his ancestors and for success against the Jin. He then returned to camp and mounted his horse, leading the Mongol army south. Having crossed the Gobi, the Mongols then rested among the Önggüd before invading the Jin Empire in May of that year. His armies broke into three groups with his sons Ögödei, Chaghadai, and Jochi taking the left wing on one route while the general Muqali, commanding the right wing, took another. Chinggis Khan commanded the center army. They captured a few cities and defeated any Jin forays sent against them, as the Mongols continued to focus their efforts along the border. By the end of 1211, the Mongols held a large swath of the Jin territory, gradually isolating the Jin capital of Zhongdu (modern Beijing). The Mongols wintered in the Jin Empire before withdrawing in February 1212, undoubtedly laden with booty. The Mongols did not annex any territory, however. Instead, they appeared content to hold the mountain passes, thus controlling the routes into the steppes and into the Jin Empire.

Peace proved short-lived, however. The Mongols resumed war in autumn, regaining any territory the Jin had recovered in their absence, including the strategic Juyong Pass, accomplished with the aid of Ja'far Khwaja, a Muslim merchant from Central Asia. He was one of the aforementioned Baljuntu, those who swore loyalty to Chinggis Khan at Lake Baljuna. As a merchant familiar with the routes between the steppes and the Jin Empire, he showed the Mongols a lesser-known route, which allowed them to take the Jin fortifications by surprise. Chinggis Khan led one army, while his son Tolui, who proved to be quite adept at war, led the other. Chinggis Khan's own army did not remain in China for long, as he suffered a wound at the siege of Xijing, causing his troops to withdraw. Still, armies led by Chinggis Khan's brother Qasar and the generals Jebe and Sübedei invaded Manchuria. The initial Mongol successes led to a few rebellions, helping to destabilize parts of the Jin Empire. Additionally, Tangut troops crossed the Xi Xia border and invaded the western portion of the Jin Empire. This allowed Chinggis Khan to recover and he return to the field in the autumn of 1213. With the return of Chinggis Khan, the Jin extended an olive branch in December. Chinggis Khan rejected it, perhaps in order to gather more plunder to make his latest invasion worthwhile.

The Mongols also continued to march on Zhongdu. The city was far too large for them to conduct a proper siege, so his armies simply blockaded it while the main army divided into three separate forces, making it difficult for the Jin to coordinate their armies.

Additionally, it forced the Jin to remain on the defensive, reacting to the attacks. The Mongols routinely defeated the field armies sent against them, before dividing their armies and raiding. The well-defended cities proved difficult as the Mongols still found siege warfare challenging. Even this, however, ceased to be an obstacle as an increasing number of Jin commanders and engineers switched sides, viewing Chinggis Khan's success as a clear sign that Heaven now favored him over the Jin Emperor. Discontented groups also rallied to the Mongols, such as Khitans, who had ruled northern China as the Liao Dynasty (906-1125) prior to the establishment of the Jin Empire. Despite the passing of almost a century, the Khitans still resented their new rulers. Try as they might, however, the Mongols could not capture Zhongdu, which probably housed more people than all of Mongolia. Eventually, peace was made in 1214, after a Jin general assassinated Emperor Yongji. As part of the treaty, the Mongols received tribute, which included a princess to be Chinggis Khan's wife with a retinue of 500 servants as well as 3000 horses, 10,000 *liang* of gold, and 10,000 bolts of silk.

The treaty of 1214 was a monumental shift in Jin policy—previously, Xi Xia, the nomads, and even the Song Empire sent tribute to the Jin Empire. Now the Jin sent a substantial sum to the Mongols. Still, while the amount was immense, it was not detrimental to Jin finances, as 10,000 *liang* of gold equals 13,330 ounces or 833 pounds, or a modern value of approximately $11.5 million. Although it may have been a sizeable amount to the Mongols, the sum was minor for the Jin. Additionally, the princess was actually the daughter of the previous emperor; thus, she would not tie the current emperor to Chinggis Khan in any sense. If anything, getting rid of the girl may have been a boon to the new Jin Emperor, as she became one less royal family member that needed maintenance. While the bride, gold, and silk were wonderful additions to Chinggis Khan's grandeur, they were minor concerns for the Jin. Nonetheless, the treaty was a blow to the Jin emperor's prestige. Losing 3000 horses, particularly as the Mongols had raided the royal studs in 1211, must have also affected the Jin's military capacity, further limiting their ability to carry out offensive actions against the Mongols, and probably why the Mongols wanted them besides replacing their own losses. The Mongols withdrew, but continued to occupy the mountain passes that led to the steppes of modern Inner Mongolia. Although they did not seek to occupy the Jin Empire, they sought to prevent the Jin from causing any problems in Mongolia.

Despite the peace, the new Emperor Xuanzong (r. 1213-1224) moved his court farther south to Kaifeng. Chinggis Khan viewed this with suspicion, and war resumed in 1215. To be fair, the Jin Emperor's move perhaps was made without malice, but out of necessity. The ravaging of the territories of Hebei, Shaanxi, and everything north of Zhongdu by the Mongols caused famine and depopulation, while leaving Zhongdu vulnerable to future attacks. This perception became reality as the Mongols invaded once more, incensed by the emperor's move. They marched directly to Zhongdu. While the Mongols still could not encircle Zhongdu, because of its size, they could blockade it with their mobility, preventing relief armies from aiding it and destroying them piecemeal. Starvation soon stalked the city while cannibalism devoured hope. Aided by these conditions, the Mongols' siege ability also improved, allowing them to breach the walls despite Zhongdu's imposing defenses. The city finally submitted in June 1215. While the conquest of the city diminished the Jin Emperor's standing, it gave Chinggis Khan his treasury but also, and perhaps of equal importance, Yelu Chucai, a Khitan who loyally served the Jin Emperor to the end as a minister of state. His loyalty to the Jin Emperor, even in defeat, impressed Chinggis Khan, who then took the tall Khitan into his own service.

The fall of Zhongdu undermined the defenses of other territories as well as the prestige of the Jin Dynasty. Rebellion broke out in several provinces as commanders and governors lost confidence in the emperor's leadership. The Khitans, who still bore grudges from the Jurchen conquest of the Liao Empire, submitted to Chinggis Khan in 1215 and proved quite useful in the conquest of north

China. Furthermore, they would play an important part in governing the new conquests. The Tanguts also initiated attacks on the western portion of the empire. Even with the fall of Zhongdu, the Jin Empire continued to resist, although the move to Kaifeng essentially conceded all of Inner Mongolia and Manchuria to the Mongols. In autumn of 1214, Chinggis Khan's brother Jochi Qasar crossed the Khingghan mountains into Manchuria and achieved the submission of the northern regions, while the general Muqali reduced the cities in southern Manchuria. With most of the Jin Empire now in Mongol hands, Chinggis Khan sent an envoy to the Jin Emperor offering him peace on the condition that the emperor present the territories of Hebei and Shandong (two areas not under Mongol control) as tribute to Chinggis Khan. Additionally, the emperor would abandon his imperial titles and assume the title of Prince of Henan, the sole province of the Mongols, would permit him to rule. Not surprisingly, Emperor Xuanzong rebuffed this audacious overture.

Thus the war continued. More Jin commanders deserted to the Mongols and more cities fell. By the fall of 1215, the Mongols held 862 walled cities (YS, 28). These concessions increasingly made the Jin's military less capable of launching offensives against the Mongols. Jin resistance nonetheless demonstrated a resilient military capacity. While the Mongols could seize the pastures of the Jin and defeat their armies, the war transformed into one of attrition as the Mongols had to conquer city by city. Leaving Muqali in charge of operations in the Jin Empire, Chinggis Khan returned to Mongolia in 1216.

More victories

Two events prevented him from turning his full attention to the Jin. The first was a rebellion in 1216 among the Hoyin Irgen, the Forest People of Siberia north of Mongolia, distracted his attention. They made efforts to resolve the issue diplomatically as Qorchi,

Chinggis Khan's governor in the region, inadvertently caused the rebellion. Qorchi, who had predicted Chinggis Khan's rise to power via the dream ox, had taken many brides, often irrespective of their previous arrangements. Naturally, this behavior caused a great deal of unrest and Botoqu Tarqun, the queen of the Qori-Tümeds, took him prisoner. Quduqa-beki, the Oirat leader, who had first opposed Chinggis Khan as part of Jamuqa's Gurkhanid confederation and then submitted to Jochi in 1207, went to negotiate on Chinggis Khan's behalf. Botoqu, however, took him prisoner as well. Chinggis Khan then dispatched his adopted brother Boroqul to quell the rebellion. An ambush in the Siberian forests brought Boroqul's life and campaign to an end. Chinggis Khan's advisors could barely restrain his anger, as Boroqul had been the foundling that Hö'elün had raised, and thus a foster brother to Chinggis Khan. Another general, Dörbei Doqshin successfully suppressed the revolt. At the same time, Jochi also marched into the Yenisei River basin to deal with the Kirghiz who had failed to send Dörbei troops—viewed as an act of rebellion. While details are scant, Jochi restored Mongol control in the Yenisei basin.

With his northern frontier secure, Chinggis Khan could now turn his attention west where other events unfolded and would result in Chinggis Khan's absence from Mongolia for approximately six years with the majority of the army. Meanwhile, his lieutenant Muqali continued to press against the Jin Empire with only a fraction of the Mongol forces. Why did Chinggis Khan abandon the Jin Campaign when the Jin were on the verge of collapse? He had little choice, as the vanity and paranoia of a ruler in Central Asia forced Chinggis Khan to take action.

During the siege of Zhongdu, a caravan from Central Asia reached Chinggis Khan's camp. Impressed by the goods as well as the merchants, he resolved to initiate commercial relations with the Khwarazmian Empire, which straddled much of Central Asia and Iran. His troops were also active in the region, pursuing those Merkit and Naiman who had yet to submit to the Mongols. The Naiman eventually encountered the empire of Qara Khitai

(1125-1218), a Buddhist Empire established in much of modern Kyrgyzstan, southern Kazakhstan, and Xinjiang by Khitan refugees from the Liao Dynasty after the Jin conquest of north China in 1125. As the Qara Khitai's halcyon days waned, the appearance of the Naiman prince Güchülüg with his troops, who had been on the run since Chakirma'ut in 1204, offered an opportunity perhaps to invigorate the empire. Zhilugu (1178-1211), the Gur Khan or Qara Khitan ruler, faced unruly vassals (such as Khwarazm to the south) and he undoubtedly had learned of the rise of Chinggis Khan. The Gur Khan gave Güchülüg refuge and married his daughter to the Naiman prince. The Christian Naiman prince converted to Buddhism in order to do so. Güchülüg's presence and rapacious behavior led many of Qara Khitai's vassals to reassess their relationship. A few, including the Uighurs, whose kingdom occupied much of the space between Xi Xia and the Tian Shan mountains, and the city of Almaliq (between the Tian Shan mountains and the Ili River, near the modern city of Yining) switched their loyalties to Chinggis Khan in 1209 and 1211 respectively, after Güchülüg passed through their territories, fleeing from the Mongols. One can suspect that Zhilugu planned to use Güchülüg to restore Uighurstan to Qara Khitan control. In return for the Gur Khan's hospitality, Güchülüg soon conspired against him and usurped the throne in 1211.

While the war against the Jin Empire and the Hoyin Irgen rebellion kept Chinggis Khan occupied, in 1216 he dispatched the general Jebe with an army to deal with the Naiman prince. Jebe augmented his troops with Uighurs and Qarluq Turks from the environs of Almaliq. Güchülüg decided the better part of valor was to flee for his life. Quite unlike the Naiman, however, the pursuing Mongols did not pillage or plunder the people of Qara Khitai. Rather, they hunted the Naiman prince. The Mongols' restraint gained them the goodwill of the populace, weary of Güchülüg's oppression. Jebe eventually ran Güchülüg to ground in Badakhshan (a region in northern Afghanistan) in 1218. He paraded Güchülug's head on a pike to show that he was truly dead, which also gives one an idea of how the populace feared Güchülüg. Jebe also took the additional step of proclaiming that all should practice their own faith and not attempt to impose it on others. (Juvaini, 67-68). This act of tolerance also highlights the religious tensions manifested during Güchülüg's reign, albeit there is evidence that the tensions had less to do with religion than with the new, higher taxes that Güchülüg imposed. That he was a Buddhist (and before that, a Christian) allowed Muslims in Qara Khitai to rationalize it as religious persecution, when in fact there is little evidence that Güchülüg allowed religion to dictate whom he oppressed, as the Uighurs were Buddhist as well. Regarding oppression, Güchülüg was an equal opportunity oppressor.

This new territorial acquisition bordered the Khwarazmian Empire, which encompassed much of modern Iran, Afghanistan, Turkmenistan, Uzbekistan, and Tajikistan, extending just north of the Syr Darya River into Kazakhstan. It was, without doubt, the strongest state within the Islamic World and territorially one of the largest empires in the world. Its ruler, Sultan Muhammad II Khwarazmshah (r. 1200-1220) viewed himself as a second Alexander the Great. Yet, despite its size, the empire was on shaky ground, as much of it Sultan Muhammad had only recently acquired. Indeed, Muhammad had been a former vassal of Qara Khitai and had conspired with Güchülüg to topple the Gur Khan. The two then fought over Mawarannahr (the territory between the Syr and Amu Darya Rivers, or roughly Uzbekistan). The caravan that Chinggis Khan encountered in Zhongdu originated from Muhammad II Khwarazmshah's territory. While the caravan returned and provided Muhammad with intelligence about Mongol activities in China, the Mongols soon sent their own caravan to establish a trade agreement with the Khwarazmian Empire.

Numbering 400 heavily laden camels and over a hundred merchants, the Mongol-sponsored caravan arrived at the frontier city of Otrar in 1218. The governor of the city determined the merchants were also spies, a not unreasonable suspicion considering that Muhammad's caravan performed the same duty. As a result, he massacred the caravan and forwarded their goods to

Sultan Muhammad. Indeed, with items such as furs from Siberia and a gold nugget the size of a camel's neck, it is reasonable to suspect that greed was the underlying factor behind the massacre. Not all were killed, however. One of the camel tenders escaped and made it back to the Mongols in Qara Khitai. They ensured that the news reached Chinggis Khan. To his credit, Chinggis Khan attempted to resolve the matter diplomatically. Sultan Muhammad, however, killed Chinggis Khan's envoy and burned the beards of his guards before sending them back to the Mongol ruler. Although Chinggis Khan had no desire to go to war in Central Asia, particularly as the Hoyin Irgen revolt had only recently abated and the Jin war continued, Muhammad's actions left him no choice.

Leaving his trusted lieutenant Muqali to conduct the Jin war, Chinggis Khan assembled an army of over 100,000 men to invade the Khwarazmian Empire. The invasion was not a surprise. For all his faults, Muhammad knew the Mongols would react, and he used his time to prepare his defenses, which included increasing the fortifications and garrisons of the cities of Mawarannahr, which lay directly in the way of the approaching Mongols. His preparations may have been enough to deal with the likes of Güchülüg or perhaps the Qangli nomads who lurked in the steppes north of the Aral Sea, but they proved woefully insufficient against the Mongols. Furthermore, while the massacred merchants may have been spies, Chinggis Khan undoubtedly knew much of Khwarazm from Ja'far, a Khwarazmian merchant who had been in Chinggis Khan's service since at least 1203. After the 1214 peace treaty with the Jin Empire, Chinggis Khan made Ja'far his *daruqachi* or governor in Mongol occupied North China. Yet Ja'far was not alone, as Chinggis Khan probably also gleaned additional information from the merchants who arrived at Zhongdu. Conversely, Muhammad Khwarazmshah also asked those merchants for information on the Mongols—considering what he heard about virgins leaping from city walls to avoid the tender embraces of the Mongol soldiery and hills of bones, he may have regretted it. (Juzjani, 964-65)

While Ögödei and Chaghadai marched on Otrar, Jochi marched

along the Syr Darya River not only to capture other cities, but also to keep the Qangli nomads who often supplied the Khwarazmshah with troops in check. Otrar fell swiftly to the Mongols. The Mongols captured the governor and then sated his avarice by pouring molten silver down his throat. While Otrar fell, the two generals Jebe and Sübedei also led their own troops in the eastern regions, including the Ferghana valley. Meanwhile, Chinggis Khan disappeared into the allegedly impenetrable Kizil Kum desert. Despite having fewer troops, the Mongols dispersal and mobility made it impossible to predict where they were heading. When Muhammad received news that Chinggis Khan appeared 300 miles behind his lines at Bukhara, it nonplussed him.

While Muhammad was dismayed, Bukhara was horrified. The city was specifically targeted by Chinggis Khan, as he learned that the loot from the massacred caravan had been stashed there. After a brief sortie by the garrison, which was destroyed, the city submitted, although the citadel held out. According to the Persian chronicler Juvaini, Chinggis Khan came to the pulpit in the great Friday Mosque before the leading men of the city and announced, "O people, know that you have committed great sins, and that the great ones among you have committed these sins. If you ask me what proof I have for these words, I say that is because I am the punishment of God. If you had not committed great sins, God would not have sent a punishment like me." (Juvaini, 105)

The city was then thoroughly plundered, and the citadel was assaulted. The Mongols rounded up the populace and determined if any were useful. The skilled artisans, particularly those who made luxury goods or armaments, were sent to Mongol camps, while the less useful ones were massacred or sent to march before the Mongols as arrow fodder. Muhammad crossed the Amu Darya and fled into Iran, in effect conceding Mawarannahr. Still, he hoped to rally against the Mongols in Khurasan.

Meanwhile, Chinggis Khan and his generals converged on Samarqand. Although defended by a large garrison, which included a contingent of war elephants, Samarqand soon fell as well—the accounts indicate it fell after five or 10 days. (Juzjani, 274, 979-980; Juvaini, 120) As with Bukhara, and as would be the trend throughout the campaign, the population was divided, with the skilled being sent to Mongol camps for labor and the unskilled marching in the front lines. Some 30,000 craftsmen from Samarqand were allegedly sent to Mongolia. (JT, 174-175; Juvaini, 120-122) Not all the Central Asians were forcibly levied to fight before the Mongols. As with the Jin Empire, many joined them willingly—everyone likes a winner. Indeed, much of the Khwarazmian Empire had only been recently conquered by Muhammad Khwarazmshah, thus only in certain regions did the populace bear him a strong allegiance.

As for Muhammad, his flight into Khurasan gave him little time to organize new resistance to the Mongols. Jebe and Sübedei did not give him such an opportunity as they pursued him through Iran and ultimately to the shores of the Caspian Sea, where he eluded them by taking a boat to an island. There, in his hubris, he died in rags, justifying his claim of being Alexander II—dying from disease rather than in battle. In their pursuit of Muhammad, however, Jebe and Sübedei took time to secure the submission of several cities. They gave the rulers a patent to show other Mongol commanders, indicating that these cities had submitted, would provide troops and provisions when requested, and thus avoid future Mongol attacks.

The wide-ranging marches of Jebe and Sübedei made the region nervous. As they approached the frontiers of the Abbasid Caliphate in Baghdad in 1222, the city prepared for war, with the Caliph al-Nasir (1180-1225) spending considerable sums on bolstering his fortifications. The Mongols never appeared, however, but continued to sweep northward into Azerbaijan. From there, they ravaged Armenia and Georgia before disappearing across the Caucasus Mountains. In the steppes north of the mountains, they engaged Alans (Iranian nomads) and Kipchak Turks, defeating them and continuing a journey of exploration. After crushing a combined force of Kipchaks and Russians at the Battle of Kalka River in 1223, during which Jebe may have died, the Mongols then returned east, crossing the Volga River and uniting with the army of Jochi, which remained in the steppes of modern Kazakhstan. This reconnaissance in force, authorized by Chinggis Khan, took a small army of fewer than 20,000 men approximately 5000 miles through unknown and hostile territory before it reunited with friendly forces—a feat that had not been duplicated.

While Jebe and Sübedei traversed Eurasia, the various Mongol armies continued their conquests in Central Asia. Chinggis Khan and Tolui arrived at Tirmiz, a city in modern Uzbekistan (Termez) and through which the Soviets invaded and then exited Afghanistan, which lay across the Amu Darya River. The Mongols quickly took this city and then divided their forces. As Chinggis Khan entered northern Afghanistan, his youngest son, Tolui, devastated Khurasan (now divided between Iran, Afghanistan, and Turkmenistan). Chroniclers wrote that even if 1000 years passed, it still would not recover. While clearly hyperbole, it remains a popular rationale of why the Islamic world lost its momentum. Nonetheless, the numerous accounts of Mongol atrocities make it clear the dramatic and traumatic effects of the Mongol onslaught, even if chroniclers exaggerated the level of destruction. Tolui was accompanied by Chinggis Khan's son-in-law, Toquchar Güregen. Toquchar, the husband of an unknown daughter of Chinggis Khan, originally had been a third commander assigned to hunting Muhammad Khwarazmshah. Unfortunately, his excessive pillaging was detrimental to the Mongols as he attacked some who had already submitted to the Mongols. As a result, Chinggis Khan stripped him of command temporarily, demonstrating that no one was exempt from scrutiny. Although he resumed leading troops in the subjugation of Khurasan, Toquchar was killed during the siege of Nishapur.

Tolui did not ignore the death of his brother-in-law, but first, he settled affairs at Merv, where he massacred the population after separating those with talents. Then he attacked Nishapur and permitted his sister to exact revenge in 1221-1222. She directed the massacre of those not deemed useful. Allegedly, Tolui also yoked oxen and ploughed the city under as well. (Juzjani, 1026-35; Juvaini,

176) With his brief foray into farming completed, Tolui then returned into modern Afghanistan and attacked the great city of Herat, which resisted valiantly for eight months before eventually being taken by the Mongols. After the sack of Herat, Tolui led his army towards Ghazna.

While Tolui laid waste to Khurasan, Chinggis Khan invaded central Afghanistan. There, Jalal al-Din, Muhammad Khwarazmshah's son and successor, sought to rally the remnants of the empire. He initially experienced some success, defeating a small army led by Shiqi Qutuqu, Chinggis Khan's foundling brother, in the Parwan Valley near Kabul. Learning of Shiqi Qutuqu's defeat, Chinggis Khan marched swiftly to Parwan. While Afghanistan has the reputation of being the Graveyard of Empires—as it is notoriously difficult to govern and pacify—Chinggis Khan's army swept across it, defeating all opposition. Jalal al-Din fled into modern Pakistan with Chinggis Khan in pursuit. Jalal al-Din only escaped by fleeing across the Indus River. The Mongols pursued briefly before withdrawing from India, finding the climate not to their or their horses' liking. Although he left a detachment to follow up against Jalal al-Din, Chinggis Khan returned to conquer Afghanistan.

Quest for immortality

While there, a Daoist sage named Changchun joined Chinggis Khan. As the master of the Quanzhen sect of Daoism, Changchun had a great deal of influence not only in the remnants of the Jin Empire, but also in the Song Empire. Yet, he developed an interest in Chinggis Khan, and when summoned to his side, the aged monk journeyed to Mongolia. However, by the time he arrived, Chinggis Khan had already departed. The monk and his entourage continued with an escort (and not always in good spirits) to join the conqueror. They finally met in Afghanistan. While Chinggis Khan enjoyed listening to Changchun's discussions of philosophy and theology, he also had a pragmatic reason for wanting Changchun by his side—he had heard that the wizened monk knew the secret to immortality. The monk said he did not, but that if Chinggis Khan would cut back on hunting, drinking, and sex, it would definitely lengthen his life span. It is doubtful that Chinggis Khan gave up all for any length of time, although after a near-death experience while hunting wild boar, he abandoned the hunt for two months. (Chih-Ch'ang, 118) While Yelu Chucai, Chinggis Khan's Khitan's advisor and devout Buddhist, worried that Chinggis Khan might convert to Quanzhen Daoism (which Yelu Chucai found bizarre), this did not happen. However, Chinggis Khan gave Changchun extensive privileges and made him the highest-ranking Daoist monk within the Mongol Empire. With this favor, Quanzhen Daoism spread rapidly through north China—even the Muslim *daruqachi* Ja'far dabbled in it and perhaps even converted to it in his old age. (Li Chih-Ch'ang, 137). After several months, Changchun returned to China where his sect of Daoism not only gained considerable influence but also was crucial in helping to restore some sense of normalcy in the wake of the Mongol destruction in the region.

Chinggis Khan's quest for immortality and his encounter with Changchun curiously contrasts with his visit by a Muslim religious authority, the *imam* and *qadi* Wahid al-Din. The latter had been at Tolui's siege of Herat. While defending the city, he fell over the wall and somehow survived. Viewing this as a miracle, Tolui sent the now captive *qadi* to Chinggis Khan, who had an interest in wise and learned men. Wahid al-Din fit the bill and for a while had Chinggis Khan's favor. One day, Chinggis Khan asked the *qadi* if the world would remember his name. Trembling, the Muslim sage bowed before him and replied, "A name continues to endure where there are people, but how will a name endure when the Khan's servants martyr all the people and massacre them, for who will remain to tell the tale?" (Juzjani 1039-42)

The response angered the Mongol leader, but he composed himself before speaking. Although Wahid al-Din thought his life was over, Chinggis Khan spared him but dismissed him from his service, saying "it has become evident to me that thou dost not possess complete understanding and that thy comprehension is but small." (Juzjani, 1042) Chinggis Khan explained that those who survived and those in neighboring kingdoms who learned of his conquests would remember him.

In 1222, Temüjin received the Jin envoy, Wugusun Zhongduan, who asked for peace. Muqali's efforts against the Jin proved to be extremely successful. The Mongols now controlled all the Jin Empire north of the Huanghe (Yellow) River. In response to the Jin, Chinggis Khan said, "Hitherto, I desired that your ruler resign to me the area north of the River, and I would give order for your ruler to be the Prince of Henan (South of the River), and you and I could call off our troops, but your ruler did not agree. Now Muqali has already taken the entire area, so why at first did you not come to sue for peace?" (YS, 35) Humbled, Wugusun Zhongduan pleaded his case and demonstrated his loyalty to the Jin Emperor by faithfully carrying out his duty as an envoy. Recognizing the difficult straits and conditions that Zhongduan was in, such as coming all the way to Central Asia to negotiate peace, Chinggis Khan agreed to terms saying, "I remember that you have come from far away; north of the River is already mine, but in Guanxi there are several cities which have not yet submitted, so give half of them to me. I will order your ruler to be the Prince of Henan, so do not defy me again." (YS, 35) The envoy dutifully returned to the Jin Emperor with the terms. Unfortunately, we have no record of the Jin Emperor's reaction to Chinggis Khan's offer. Events unfolded that made the situation moot, however.

Conquests continue

While still in Central Asia, word soon reached Chinggis Khan that not only did Muqali die in 1223, but also Xi Xia took his absence and Muqali's death as a sign to rebel. The Jin Emperor Xuanzong (r.1213-1224) died in the same year. Leaving the Khwarazmian Empire in smoldering ruins, Chinggis Khan departed north in 1225. The previous year, he had entered India, contemplating returning to his domains via a southern route through Tibet. He encountered a unicorn (probably a rhinoceros) in India. The event was taken as an inauspicious sign and he returned to Afghanistan, summering there before returning north. Despite destroying the empire, the Mongols only retained Mawarannahr, leaving a *daruqachi*, or governor, with a body of troops. It was not a large force as it was not needed; the Khwarazmian defeat was complete. Chinggis Khan led the rest of the army back to Mongolia.

He attempted to resolve the Xi Xia incident diplomatically. The Tangut simply needed to come and submit to him and leave hostages. The return from Central Asia was long, so they had time to consider Chinggis Khan's terms. Rather than go directly to Xi Xia, he returned first to Mongolia to rest his men. *The Secret History* reported that the ruler of Xi Xia had refused to supply troops for the Khwarazmian campaign. (SHM, 256) As noted earlier, the Mongols viewed the refusal to supply provisions, troops, or appear before the ruler, as sedition. From the Hoyin Irgen rebellion, the Mongols dealt with rebellions swiftly and decisively. Considering that this ostensibly took place in 1218 or 1219 at the latest, it does not seem plausible that Chinggis Khan would have left a rebellion unattended for five years and there are no reports that any other general was assigned to deal with it. In reality, the Tangut continued to provide troops against the Jin Empire. It was not until late 1222 or 1223 that the Tangut rebelled, after the Jin had a successful counterattack against the Mongols. They deserted Muqali at a siege in Shaanxi. While Muqali prosecuted a war of punishment against the Tangut, he died on April 1223 before completing it. His lieutenants could not effectively continue the campaign as the Jin, then took advantage of the situation and pressed the remaining Mongol forces in north China. Muqali's son Bol eventually returned to Xi Xia, quelled the rebellion, and the Tangut Ruler Li Zunxu (r. 1211-1223) abdicated. His son, Li Dewang (1223-1226), waited until Bol had departed and then rebelled again. Thus, this often-cited reason does not hold water, unless it is referring to a request from Muqali for troops, as Xi Xia provided soldiers in 1216 and 1221. The Tangut, however, picked an opportune time to rebel. With Muqali's army stretched thin on two fronts (Xi Xia and the Jin Empire) and while Chinggis Khan was over 1000 miles away in modern Afghanistan, a better opportunity could not have materialized. The Tangut, however, sadly miscalculated Chinggis Khan's intent.

After Mongol forces took the city of Yinzhou in eastern Xi Xia, Li Dewang sued for peace. Chinggis Khan, still in Central Asia, accepted the peace overtures but demanded a hostage to ensure good behavior. The Tangut ruler proved to be perfidious and pursued an alliance with the Jin Empire in 1224. Thus, when Chinggis Khan returned to Mongolia, he did not find a hostage waiting for him, but discovered instead that the Tangut had rebelled yet again. The timing was perfect. Not only did the Mongols face a resurgent Jin Empire, but Mongol troops had also engaged the Song Empire in skirmishes, as the latter also attempted to claim Jin territory occupied by the Mongols. The Song viewed it as rightfully theirs, since the Jin had conquered it from the Song Empire earlier. Finally, Chinggis Khan still had a vast swath of Central Asian territory to incorporate into his empire. Yet, rather than deal with these issues, he focused on the recalcitrant Tangut, although Chinggis Khan sent his sons Ögödei and Chaghadai in 1226 to attack the Jin and revitalize Mongol efforts there, and probably to prevent the Jin and Tangut from coordinating their efforts against him.

Having rested, a Mongol army left Chinggis Khan's camp on the Tula River in November 1225 and marched towards Xi Xia. The invasion did not begin until March 1226, with the Mongols having to rebuild bridges that Xi Xia's military destroyed. City after city fell to the invading Mongols. Amid these conquests, Li Dewang died, leaving his younger brother, Li Xian (r. 1226-1227) to clean up his mess. Xi Xia did not defeat Chinggis Khan on the battlefield, having learned it was useless. Instead, they hoped the Mongols would wear themselves out against the Xi Xia cities, and perhaps either settle for plunder or create an opening for a counterattack. With no opposition before them, the main Mongol army divided and continued to reduce the Tangut defenses throughout 1226, capturing Lingzhou, south of the Tangut capital of Zhongxing.

In January 1227, the Mongols attacked the capital of Zhongxing, laying siege to the city. With Li Xian bottled up in the city and with no relief on the horizon, Chinggis Khan relaxed and went hunting. During the process, the sudden appearance of *qulan* (wild asses) startled his horse, flinging the Mongol leader. During his recovery from the sustained injuries, he ordered his sons and generals not to reveal his condition to anyone but continue to press the siege. One of his servitors, Tolun-cherbi (his chamberlain) suggested that they withdraw to Mongolia so he could recover better. He pointed out that the Tangut lived in cities and would go nowhere—the Mongols could return when they wanted and finish the job.

Chinggis Khan refused because it would only encourage the Tangut. He ordered his armies to press the attack: "The Tang'ut people will say that we turned back because we lost heart." (SHM, §265) Meanwhile, the Mongol armies defeated the Tangut general Asa Gambu, who had encouraged the rebellion. The decree that Chinggis Khan ordered after the Mongol victory made his intent clear. He ordered, "Kill the valiant, the bold, the manly and the fine Tang'uts, and let the soldiers take for themselves as many of the common Tang'uts as they can lay hands on and capture." (SHM, §265) In this decree, Chinggis Khan has ordered his army to attack and kill all who oppose them. Those who surrender would be enslaved and dispersed among the Mongol people. Understanding that the Tangut elite would never accept Mongol rule, Chinggis Khan ordered a genocide to resolve the rebellion.

The Mongols continued to reduce all outlying strongholds. As they continued their siege, Li Xian requested an audience and brought tribute to make peace. In his stricken condition, Chinggis Khan refused to meet with him, but allowed the Tangut leader to grovel outside his *ger*. Chinggis Khan had determined that he wanted the Tangut leader killed. Tolun-cherbi carried out the order and suffocated the Tangut leader. Yet, Chinggis Khan's condition did not improve. The injuries from his fall were too severe, and he appears to have been aware that he was not long for this world. Even though he was on his deathbed, Chinggis Khan insisted that the Mongols continue their assault and ordered his sons and generals, "While I take my meals you must talk about the killing and destruction of the Tang'ut and say, 'Maimed and tamed, they are no more.'" (SHM, §268).

Although he died on August 18, 1227, his commanders carried out his order faithfully. Zhongzhou was sacked, and the Tangut royal family massacred. Not all of the Tangut were killed, but the kingdom of Xi Xia disappeared. The Tangut people were dispersed among the Mongols, and many of them went to Yisüi, one of Chinggis Khan's Tatar wives who accompanied him on the campaign and attended him during his illness. It remains unknown where the Mongols buried Chinggis Khan, despite many efforts to find his grave. Tolui, his youngest son by Börte, served as regent until 1229, when Ögödei assumed the throne as the second ruler of the Mongol Empire.

6. Family Matters

As the saying goes, you can pick your friends, but you cannot choose your family. This chapter explores Chinggis Khan's relationship with his family members in more depth. Chinggis Khan elevated his family to the status of royalty and installed safeguards to protect them. He also instituted a system of checks and balances to ensure that his relatives could not challenge his authority, as it is apparent that he did not fully trust them. At the same time, with the creation of the *altan urugh* or Golden Kin, as the Chinggisid family became known, a new royalty came into existence that influenced events in Eurasia for several hundred years. The last Chinggisid ruler, Muhammad Alim Khan of Bukhara, only vacated his throne in 1920 due to the rise of communism in the Soviet Union, which "Sovietized" Mongolia. Additionally, the *altan urugh* provided a network to rule the empire, whether through the sons and grandsons, the daughters, and even sons-in-law. The Mongol Empire was very much a family-run business. While other institutions existed and contributed to the administration of the empire, the *altan urugh* was unquestionably the primary means of governance. Although Chinggis Khan kept the *altan urugh* under control, he also established it so that other lineages could not possibly consider themselves above the *altan urugh*. Of course, a major factor in this was the prestige of Chinggis Khan, which gave unrivaled legitimacy to his family's claim to power.

With Yisügei's death, Chinggis Khan's most immediate family was his mother and siblings, including his half-brothers Bekter and Belgütei. As mentioned earlier, the young Temüjin, with the aid of his younger brother Jochi Qasar, murdered their elder half-brother Bekter as the latter stole food. This incident is only recorded in *The Secret History of the Mongols*, which laconically details Chinggis Khan's faults as much as it also indulges in hagiographic praise.

Yet this scenario is more than simply sibling rivalry and unchecked anger. Bekter's theft of food did more than risk the welfare of the family—it also demonstrated how an individual placed his own welfare above that of his family. As discussed previously, the fratricide also prevented the possibility of Bekter marrying Hö'elün, Temüjin's mother. Steppe tradition allowed the possibility of a relative, including sons, to marry their stepmothers. There were several reasons for this. The economic reason was to keep the dowry and wife's property within the family. Secondly, on a more practical level, and considering the low population density among the nomads, it also eased the task of attempting to find another husband and allowed the family unit to continue with its division of labor. Thus, the murder prevented Bekter from assuming the patriarch position of the family. We will never know what Hö'elün would have thought of the idea of marriage. Her reaction to the murder, as recorded in *The Secret History of the Mongols*, suggests that she was at least not completely opposed to the idea, but the murder genuinely horrified her. One must remember that she did not marry Yisügei out of love—they kidnapped her while traveling to her original Merkit husband's pastures. Under these circumstances, the option of marrying her stepson may have seemed reasonable, though likely odd to the modern reader.

The murder propelled Temüjin to the top of the male hierarchy in his family. Clearly, his mother still wielded authority and influence—by the time of Bekter's death, Temüjin was not even a teenager. Still, as he aged, he gradually assumed the mantle of leadership. When the family's horses were stolen, he was the one to pursue the thieves, even though it was Belgütei who returned from hunting with their remaining horse.

Jochi Qasar was the next eldest brother, and Temüjin's co-conspirator against Bekter. In many ways, Jochi Qasar became the muscle behind Temüjin's schemes. While Temüjin shot and killed Bekter from behind, Jochi Qasar shot him from the front. Their attack ensured that Bekter could not escape. When the Tayichi'ud attacked, Jochi Qasar was the one who kept the Tayichi'ud at bay with his archery skills, eventually becoming a renowned archer and warrior. Early on, Qasar often accompanied Temüjin or served as his envoy. However, there are some signs that Qasar's archery skills caused tension between the two brothers and they were not always on good terms. Indeed, in 1203 Jochi Qasar was with the Kereit, although he eventually joined Temüjin. It is not clear why he was there, whether it was his own choice, whether he served Toghril directly as a *nökör*, or perhaps even as a hostage. At the 1206 *quriltai*, Chinggis Khan allotted him 4000 people, fewer than he gave his sons. Later tensions became even more apparent when a shaman suggested that Jochi Qasar would eventually replace Chinggis Khan as the leader of the Mongols.

Like Temüjin's younger sister Temülün, Börte's third son Qachi'un received little attention in the *Secret History of the Mongols* beyond the mention of his birth; even less attention is paid to him in other sources. We know he existed but have little knowledge of what he did. One gets the sense that this middle child possessed a less dominant personality and preferred to assist rather than lead. Indeed, considering the staggering talent of Temüjin and the prowess of Jochi Qasar, one can see why he might have lacked the same level of confidence. There is no indication that he received an allotment of people, so perhaps he died before 1206, or maybe much earlier.

Temüjin's relationship with his stepbrother Belgütei was interesting. Before he died, Bekter asked Temüjin to spare Belgütei, his younger brother. Temüjin consented, and he and Belgütei developed a strong bond that was not adversely affected by the fratricide. One might wonder if guilt strengthened Temüjin's affection for Belgütei. He became a trusted councilor and given responsibility, although one must wonder if Temüjin's trust in Belgütei's abilities was warranted. Belgütei, it must be remembered, was wounded in the Jürkin brawl. However, he got his revenge by breaking the spine of his assailant in a wrestling match. That Temüjin fixed the match does not matter—he could have chosen anyone to wrestle. In medieval Mongolia, as today, wrestling was considered one of the three manly sports, archery and horse racing being the others. The vengeance aspect of this incident is important, but one cannot ignore that Chinggis Khan placed his brother in a position to succeed and play an important role, including that of executioner. Belgütei, however, had his faults as well. While supervising the captivity of the Tatars after their defeat, Belgütei let it slip that they were probably going to be executed. This led to active resistance by the prisoners and the wounding of several Mongols. After this event, they did not include Belgütei in the counsels. His lack of discretion proved to Chinggis Khan that they could rely on him to carry out orders, but not to be trusted with confidential matters. Temüjin, however, permitted him to serve as a judge over minor offenses. In 1206, Temüjin allotted 1500 people to him.

Temüge was the youngest of Chinggis Khan's brothers. He appeared to lack the gravitas of Temüjin and Jochi Qasar. As the youngest, his initial deficiency of determination and charisma may have been simply due to his youth. He took part in the unification of Mongolia and was present at the battle of Chakirma'ut, in charge of the rearguard. This might seem like a relatively unimportant position, but it actually was key, considering the mobility of nomadic armies. Protecting the rear was essential, as encirclement was a frequent risk and the rear guard had the role of filling gaps and launching counterattacks in case the main body was forced back. Still, it took assistance from Temüjin to develop Temüge's strength of character, which seemingly came so naturally to Temüjin. It occurred, and Temüjin gradually trusted Temüge with great responsibilities. He served as regent when Chinggis Khan went on campaign and ruled in his stead. Chinggis Khan's trust in his youngest brother was well placed. When he departed for the Khwarazmian campaign, Chinggis Khan remained outside of Mongolia for six years. Although Xi Xia rebelled (and only after the death of the nearest military commander, Muqali), Mongolia remained stable and the cornerstone of the empire. There is no indication that Temüge ever sought to usurp the throne. Indeed, it appears he only actively thought about taking the throne after the death of Ögödei, Chinggis Khan's son and successor, and this was only four or five years after Ögödei's death when the throne sat vacant. (Juvaini, 244) While he contemplated a coup, he ultimately withdrew. A lateral succession was not out of the question as it was a common practice among the Central Eurasian nomads. Unfortunately for him, the eventual successor, Güyük (Ögödei's son) viewed Temüge's actions as a threat and had him executed, ending the possibility of the throne ever going to one of the families of Chinggis Khan's brother.

Temüjin's uncles

Although uncle Daritai's role in elevating Temüjin as Khan and his later betrayal of Temüjin have been discussed, there are other aspects of Temüjin's relationship with his uncles that merit attention. Yisügei had three brothers; two older ones named Monggetü Kiyan and Nekün Taisi, while Daritai Otchigin was the youngest, as evinced by the Otichigin title: Otchigin means the one who inherited the hearth (meaning the camp) of his father. Of these four sons of Bartan Ba'atar (Chinggis Khan's grandfather), Mönggetü Kiyan disappeared from history early. He is only mentioned once in *The Secret History of the Mongols*. (SHM, §50) His son, Önggür however, became a commander of a *minggan* and one of Chinggis Khan's cooks; he also had a seat of honor in the presence of Chinggis Khan, next to his son Tolui. While it may seem a menial position, the cook had direct access to Chinggis Khan and thus could poison him. As a result, only a trusted individual could hold that position. As for Nekün, Taisi and Daritai, they assisted Yisügei in absconding with Hö'elün. Indeed, as they returned to Yisügei's camp, Daritai was the one who told Hö'elün to forget Chiledü, her Merkit husband, as he has fled and would never come back for her:

> The one who held you in his arms
> Has *already* crossed many ridges;
> The one you bewail
> Has *already* crossed many streams.
> If you call him, and he looks back,
> He will not see you;
> If you look for his tracks,
> His trail you will not find.
> Be quiet! (SHM, §56)

While not the most comforting, Daritai and his brother helped to bring Yisügei and Hö'elün together. Afterwards, they disappeared from the sources, but we must not conclude that they also disappeared from Yisügei's family's life. Still, they are not mentioned in connection with Yisügei's death or with the ostracization of Hö'elün and his children at the *quriltai*. Why did neither marry Hö'elün? Indeed, Daritai did not appear again until Temüjin's adulthood. Daritai was among those who joined Temüjin after he separated from Jamuqa, thus indicating that Daritai was part of Jamuqa's following. *The Secret History* only mentions Nekün Taisi once more, and in passing during the feast that led to the Jürkin brawl. In this, it is stated that he was dead. (SHM, §130) It is not clear when he died, but as the events with the Jürkin took place after Jamuqa defeated Temüjin, he may have passed away during Temüjin's exile.

While Daritai's relationship with Temüjin became strained, Temüjin initially held him in respect. During the battle of Köyiten between Jamuqa's Gur-Khanid confederation against Toghril and Temüjin, Daritai (along with Altan and Quchar) was given command of the vanguard—a position of honor. Perhaps this elevated position made Daritai and the others believe they could then ignore the "Thou shalt not plunder" edict when they fought the Tatars in 1202. While Temüjin confiscated the plunder, it did not lead to an immediate rupture between uncle and nephew, but Daritai's stature diminished in Temüjin's eyes. Indeed, after this event, Daritai, like

Belgütei, was no longer admitted into Temüjin's council. The exclusion from Temüjin's company was not total, however. After Temüjin and his advisors completed their meetings, Daritai, like Belgütei, could then join his nephew for a round of drinking and socializing. It is clear, however, that Daritai had lost Temüjin's trust. His disdain for Daritai only intensified after his uncle joined Toghril and conspired against him. During the *quriltai* that elevated Temüjin as Chinggis Khan, he rewarded his supporters, including his family. Even a few years after the defeat and incorporation of the Kereit into the *Yeke Monggol Ulus*, he had not forgiven his uncle saying "I shall destroy [him] out of the sight of the eyes." His trusted companions, Muqali, Bo'orchu, and his foster-brother Shiqi Qutuqu, cautioned him against it, saying:

> This action would be
> Like extinguishing one's own *hearth*-fire,
> Like destroying one's own tent. (SHM, §242)

They then advised him to let him live for the sake of the memory of his father, Yisügei. Thus, Chinggis Khan spared Daritai's life, and his uncle faded from memory.

The foundlings

Besides his immediate family tied through Yisügei, Chinggis Khan had four adopted relatives. Depending on the source, they are depicted as either sons or brothers. I view them as brothers, as these "foundlings" were given to Hö'elün to care for. She raised them to be loyal to her sons and serve as their eyes and ears. These were not just orphans, but children who became orphans because of Chinggis Khan. Each came from a tribe that Chinggis Khan defeated during his rise to power. In order of acquisition, they were Küchü of the Merkit, Kököchü of the Besüd, Shiqi Qutuqu of the Tatars, and Boroqul of the Jürkin.

Küchü, also known as Güchü, is a lesser-known "foundling" but the first to enter Hö'elün's care. She acquired him during Temüjin's rescue of Börte. When the Merkit fled their camp during the rescue operation, Mongol warriors found the boy. Judging by his clothing, he was probably the child of someone important:

> At the time when the Uduyit Merkit were fleeing in haste, our soldiers found a little boy of five with fire in his eyes who had been left behind in the camp and whose name was Kücü. He had a sable cap, boots made from *the skin of* a doe's forelegs, and a dress of otter skins cleared of hair and sewn together. They took him and brought him to Mother Hö'elün, and gave him to her as a present. (SHM, §114)

This passage reveals much. The details of his clothing, such as the sable cap, identify him as a child of an aristocrat. Normally, the Secret Historian does not describe ubiquitous items such as clothing, so the fact that he did indicates that this person was of significance. Additionally, the reference to a "fire in his eyes" is a way that Dei Sechen referred to Temüjin in his youth. (SHM, §138) It is a reference to having innate greatness.

Obviously, this quality was not on a par with that of Chinggis Khan, but he gave his adopted brother the command of 1000 men among the people assigned to Hö'elün, thus maintaining a vital connection to Küchü. This was not simply a matter of having Hö'elün monitor the Merkit. Chinggis Khan assigned his mother and younger brother Temüge Otchigin 10,000 men. Küchü, along with four others, were to serve as commanders of those troops and as advisors to Temüge. Küchü's fellow "foundling" Kököchü joined him in this capacity. Indeed, their gratitude and loyalty towards Hö'elün were manifested in important matters. When Chinggis Khan came to interrogate his brother Jochi Qasar over his alleged plans for a coup (as will be discussed), they quickly informed mother Hö'elün. Even though she traveled through the night, she arrived before Chinggis Khan could do anything too rash. (SHM, §243, 244) There is no indication that Chinggis Khan retaliated against Küchü or Kököchü.

Kököchü entered the family when Temüjin broke with Jamuqa. Temüjin's path went through the pastures of the Tayichi'ud. The sudden appearance of Temüjin with his followers caught the Tayichi'ud by surprise, causing them to leave their camp for fear of attack. Among the abandoned camp, his scouts found a small child from the Besüd Mongols (a segment of the Tayichi'ud). He was brought back and entered the care of Hö'elün. This child, Kököchü, served Chinggis Khan well. At the *quriltai* of 1206, Chinggis Khan made him one of the commanders of a *minggan* and an advisor to Temüge.

Although Küchü and Kököchü both served Chinggis Khan and his mother commendably, their story ends there. A third foundling named Shiqi Qutuqu, however, became a key member of the Mongol government. Like Küchü, Shiqi Qutuqu appears to have been the son of an aristocrat. Mother Hö'elün took him in after the joint force of Mongols, and Jin troops defeated the Tatars in 1196-97. They found the child wearing a gold ring in his nose and a sash of gold silk lined with sable around his waist, which also demonstrates the wealth of the Tatars vis-à-vis the Merkit—proximity to the Jin made a difference. While Hö'elün raised all the foundlings, *The Secret History* refers to Shigi Qutuqu as Hö'elün's sixth son (after the five sons of Yisügei, although Yisügei actually had six sons). (SHM, §135) Like the rest of the foundlings, he became a commander of a *minggan*.

Shiqi Qutuqu also had a feisty side and would not let his comparable youth be seen as a detriment. After the assigning of commanders to the *minggans*, Chinggis Khan instructed Shiqi Qutuqu to call for his two senior commanders, Muqali and Bo'orchu, so he could grant them favors. Shiqi Qutuqu questioned his adopted brother about how these men had provided more service than he had. He reminded his brother that from his childhood until now he had served both Chinggis Khan and his mother dutifully and concluded with, "Now, what kind of reward will you give me?" (SHM, §203)

Perhaps, pleased with Shiqi Qutuqu self-confidence, Chinggis Khan acknowledged him as his sixth brother and granted him freedom from punishment for nine transgressions. Additionally, he assigned Shiqi Qutuqu the task of apportioning the people among his family. Furthermore, he made Shiqi Qutuqu the *yeke jarquchi*, or chief judge, as well as the holder of the *Köke Debter*, or Blue Book, the register in which the edicts of Chinggis Khan were written. Thus, not only did he serve as judge, but also as the recorder of law. These positions placed him on a par with Muqali and Bo'orchu in terms of counsel. Along with those two, Shiqi Qutuqu convinced Chinggis Khan not to execute his uncle Daritai. Shiqi Qutuqu was also instrumental in persuading Chinggis Khan to be lenient with his sons Ögödei, Chaghadai, and Jochi when the three quarreled during the Khwarazmian campaign.

Chinggis Khan's trust in his sixth brother was well placed. In 1215, when the Mongols conquered Zhongdu, they also captured the emperor's treasury. While some commanders wanted to help themselves to a part of the loot, as surely there was more than enough, Shiqi Qutuqu was steadfast in his opposition. He informed them that as the treasury was once the possession of the Jin Emperor, it now belonged to Chinggis Khan. While Chinggis Khan rebuked those who had been tempted, he praised Shiqi Qutuqu, saying:

> Shalt thou not be
> Mine eyes for seeing,
> Mine ears for hear? (SHM, §252)

While he earned Chinggis Khan's trust and admiration, being included in the same counsels as Bo'orchu and Muqali, he lacked their military ability. Shiqi Qutuqu proved to be an adequate commander, but not a great general. During the Khwarazmian campaign, Jalal al-Din defeated him in the Parwan Valley, near Kabul. Yet, his defeat came while he led the vanguard of Chinggis

Khan, a position of honor. Furthermore, while beaten, Shiqi Qutuqu's defeat was not a rout, as the Khwarazmians withdrew upon Chinggis Khan's approach.

The final foundling, Boroqul of the Jürkin, rose to become one of Chinggis Khan's most trusted men, more so than any of his actual brothers. Chinggis Khan praised Boroqul for being swift in warfare, for sheltering him from rain, and providing broth in the cold while on campaign. These were perhaps minor favors, but Boroqul dutifully kept an eye on the welfare of his foster brother. Boroqul's wife, Altani, saved the life of Chinggis Khan's son, Tolui, when a Tatar prisoner attempted to murder the boy. She raised the alarm. Chinggis Khan also noted how Boroqul saved the life of his son Ögödei, who had been wounded in the neck during the battle against the Kereit. Boroqul not only rescued him, but sucked on the wound to prevent a clot from forming. Chinggis Khan fully recognized that if his mother had not raised Boroqul, he would have lost two of his sons. As a reward, Chinggis Khan rewarded him by stating "If Boroqul commits *up* to nine crimes he shall not be punished." (SHM, §172-73, 213,214) In essence, Chinggis Khan indicated that thanks to his service, Boroqul could do no wrong.

Yet this is not all that Boroqul did. He also proved to be a capable military leader, and he won the respect of Chinggis Khan as a *minggan* commander, a warrior, and leader. Chinggis Khan made him one of his *Dörben Külü'üd*, or four steeds—an elite brigade ostensibly comprising four *minggans*, each commanded by a different steed (Bo'orchu, Muqali, and Chila'un were the other three). They were assigned the difficult tasks, such as when the Naiman trapped Toghril after he deserted Temüjin, who, in turn, dispatched the *Dörben Külü'üd* to Toghril's aid, and they rescued Senggüm. Furthermore, Boroqul joined Önggür in becoming one of Chinggis Khan's cooks, elevating him even higher in the court. Like Önggür, he sat next to Tolui in a position of honor.

Despite his position of cook in Chinggis Khan's household, Boroqul's military responsibilities did not end. When the Hoyin Irgen rebelled, Boroqul led the army to deal with them.

Unfortunately, the Qori Tümed killed him in an ambush as he scouted the route with a small party. His death angered Chinggis Khan. Only the counsel of his oldest friend Bo'orchu and leading general Muqali prevented Chinggis Khan from leading the campaign against the Qori Tümed. If he had, his affection for Boroqul would have likely meant the extermination of the Qori Tümed. Instead, he assigned Dörbei Doqshin to subdue the enemy.

More family connections: Mönglik

Besides his brothers by birth, Belgütei, and the foundlings, Chinggis Khan also had new stepbrothers, as Hö'elün eventually remarried. It is not clear when she remarried, but she did after her sons had attained adulthood. Her new husband was Mönglik, the son of Charaqa of the Qongqotan, a *nökör* of Yisügei. One may recall Charaqa died at the hands of the Tayichi'ud when they took Yisügei's people after his death. Mönglik also played an important role at the time of Yisügei's death. While Yisügei lay dying from the Tatar's poison, he gave Mönglik instructions:

> Mönglik my boy, I have young children. I left my son Temüjin to be a son-in-law and, as I was coming back, I was secretly harmed by Tatar people on the way. I feel sick within me. You take care of your younger brothers, the little ones that I leave behind, and of your widowed elder sister-in-law. Go quickly and bring back my son Temüjin, Mönglik my boy! (SHM, §68)

From this passage, we can glean that Mönglik (and thus his father Charaqa) had a familial connection to Yisügei, but that Mönglik was significantly younger than Yisügei, albeit still an adult, as one would not send a young child on such a mission. Not only did Yisügei's last will and testament instruct Mönglik to retrieve Temüjin, but also to assist in the care of Yisügei's children and help his "elder sister-in-law" who was a widow. This can only mean Hö'elün, implying that Mönglik was the younger brother of Yisügei's other wife, Süchigil. and thus the uncle of Bekter and Belgütei. It also means that Charaqa's death was not simply about protecting Yisügei's family, but also about Charaqa's daughter and his own grandchildren.

Mönglik certainly fulfilled Yisügei's last request in retrieving Temüjin. It is clear that Mönglik and Charaqa initially stayed with Yisügei's family. When the Taychi'ud tried to take Yisügei's people with them after the *quriltai*, Charaqa was one who opposed them and the Tayichi'ud literally stabbed him in the back for his efforts. His death affected Temüjin, who had to leave the *ger* to weep when someone brought Charaqa's body into the tent. This may have also been the first violent death that Temüjin witnessed. Mönglik, however, did not resist like his father.

Indeed, Mönglik apparently also abandoned his sister- and sister-in-law and departed. He was not present in their lives until after Dalan Baljut, and did not appear again until Temüjin's return from exile. Mönglik, along with several others, left Jamuqa and joined Temüjin. Considering that Yisügei had charged Mönglik with taking care of his family after his death, Mönglik's absence in the sources is surprising. Yet, once he returned to Temüjin's service, he proved his worth and loyalty. When Toghril and Senggüm suddenly agreed that Jochi could marry Cha'ur, Mönglik questioned the Kereit's motives, even before the Kereit grooms warned Chinggis Khan. Mönglik asked, "When we requested [Cha'ur] Beki, those same *people* despised us and would not provide her. How is it that now, on the contrary, they invite you to dine at the betrothal feast? Why do people who think themselves *so* important invite you, and contradicting themselves, *now* say 'We shall provide her'? Are they right? Are they correct?" (SHM §168)

This passage reveals a few pieces of information as well. It is likely that, at this point, Mönglik and Hö'elün were married. The Secret Historian refers to Mönglik as Father Mönglik (*Echige* Mönglik), but this is not surprising, as even in the scenes where Temüjin is nine years old and Mönglik relatively young, he is referred to as Father

Mönglik, indicating his future status. Mönglik refers to Temüjin as "son." It may simply be an elder speaking to a younger man, but it seems unlikely. So where was Hö'elün in this discussion? It is not clear, but most likely she had her own tent. There is also the equal possibility that she was at a separate camp and not married. I suspect she may have remarried after all the foundlings became adults, although some suggest that she married shortly after the debacle at Dalan Baljut.

Mönglik's status was further clarified at the *quriltai* of 1206 when he was given command of a *minggan*; indeed, he is the first one named. His son, Tolun. also received a command and along with his brother Söyiketü, became one of Chinggis Khan's six chamberlains (who managed his household and staff) as well. Mönglik's received additional awards and we learn he had assisted Chinggis Khan on a number of occasions that are not mentioned in *The Secret History of the Mongols*. Chinggis Khan said:

> You fortunate and blessed *man*
> Who at birth were born *with me*,
> When growing, grew up together *with me*,
> How many times have you helped and protected me?"
> (SHM, §204)

Additionally, he stated that Mönglik would always be appreciated and remembered. Chinggis Khan also informed Mönglik that he would receive gifts every month and they would continue on to his descendants. Furthermore, he gave Mönglik a seat of honor on the corner of the throne—a symbolic way of stating that he was close to the Khan. (SHM, §204) Yet, the above passage is curious, as it states that they might have been closer in age than one would guess. However, we should not read too much into it, as it is simply a way of saying that they have known each other since Chinggis Khan's childhood; the same phrasing is used with Jelme, who came into Chinggis Khan's life much later than Mönglik. (SHM, §211) Although the sources do not mention Mönglik during the period between the ostracism and Temüjin's marriage, perhaps Mönglik was present occasionally. As I indicated earlier, the *Secret History* encourages the reader to believe that the family was completely abandoned and isolated. Yet, at various times this ruse is revealed, albeit subtly.

Although Chinggis Khan honored Mönglik, his esteem waned due to the actions of his sons. By 1206, Hö'elün and Mönglik were married, thus making him Chinggis Khan's stepfather. Of greater importance was that Mönglik had his own seven sons from another wife or more. Kököchü (not to be confused with the "foundling" Kököchü), his fourth and thus the true middle child, emerged as the most ambitious of the seven. Kököchü is better known by his shamanic name, Teb Tenggeri—loosely translated, this means Most Heavenly. Able to commune with the spirit world and Möngke Köke Tenggeri (the Eternal Blue Sky), Teb Tenggeri informed all that Heaven had given Temüjin the earth and that he would rule as Chinggis Khan. (JT, 263)

Teb Tenggeri's sons became stepbrothers through the marriage of Mönglik and Hö'elün. The honor given to Mönglik and Chinggis Khan's wariness towards his own brothers also gave these sons an over-inflated sense of importance. Indeed, at one point they beat up Jochi Qasar and took some of his people. Teb Tenggeri also played on Chinggis Khan's insecurities and told the Mongol leader of a portent he experienced, "The decree of Eternal Heaven *concerning* the ruler has been *foretold* by *heavenly* signs as *follows*: once they say that Temüjin will hold the nation, once that Qasar *will*." (SHM, §244) He then advised that Temüjin needed to deal with Jochi Qasar immediately, before the latter took the throne. Swayed by the shaman's words, Chinggis Khan did so, but fortunately, the foundlings Kököchü and Küchü warned Hö'elün of this event. Her intervention may have saved Jochi Qasar's life, although she did not spare Chinggis Khan from a public berating that would put anyone to shame—she pulled out her breasts and told them how they used to suckle and other moments of their childhood. One may wonder what Hö'elün thought of Mönglik's sons after this. Despite being humbled, Chinggis Khan still punished Jochi Qasar by taking many of his people from him, leaving him with a scant 1400 followers.

Saddened by this, Hö'elün suffered from depression and her health declined.

Teb Tenggeri was not finished yet. He and his brothers also targeted Temüge, roughing him up and taking some of his people (who also belonged to Hö'elün). Furthermore, they made him kneel before Teb Tenggeri. One may suspect that he and his brothers believed her people should belong to their father as well. This time, Börte intervened when Temüge petitioned his brother to deal with the issue. Börte asked him, if Mönglik's sons can do this to his brothers while he is alive, what will they do to his sons when he dies? (SHM, §245) This got Chinggis Khan's attention, and he arranged a meeting.

Mönglik and his seven sons came into Chinggis Khan's *ger*. Temüge immediately grabbed the shaman by the collar, and the two struggled. Chinggis Khan ordered the two of them to settle it outside. The others remained inside. After Teb Tenggeri exited, three of Temüge's henchmen grabbed him and broke his spine, disposing of the body at the edge of the camp. Temüge returned and said, "Teb Tenggeri had compelled me to make amends. When I said, 'Let us measure up to each other', he was not willing *to wrestle* and lay down, pretending *that he could not get up*. Not much of a companion, is he!" (SHM, §245) Mönglik quickly realized what happened and started to weep, saying

> I have been your companion
> Since the brown earth
> Was *only* the size of a clod,
> Since the sea and rivers
> Were *only* the size of a rivulet. SHM, §245

Mönglik was obviously distraught and amazed that Chinggis Khan had his son killed. Meanwhile, his remaining sons stood and rolled their sleeves up, intimidating Chinggis Khan. With no guards inside (not unusual), he quickly stood up and said, "make way." His status and presence of command made the sons pause. Exiting safely, his guards took care of the rest. He properly disposed of Teb Tenggeri's body and then chastised Mönglik with the intensity of Al Pacino saying, "By not restraining your sons' nature, you *and your sons* began thinking that you were equal to *me*, and you have paid *for this* with Teb Tenggeri's life. If I had known that you had such a nature, you would have been dealt with like Jamuqa, Altan, Quchar, and others." (SHM, §246) After he calmed down, Chinggis Khan forgave Mönglik and considered the matter over. Thus, while Mönglik retained his status and the monthly gifts, he no longer had Chinggis Khan's trust or esteem. His remaining sons ceased to be a problem. Indeed, Tolan became a commander and figure of exceptional ability in the empire's rise. One can expect, however, that if Mönglik's sons had not toed the line afterwards, they too would have to be executed.

The Khan's children

Chinggis Khan's relationship with his children influenced and shaped the structure of the Mongol Empire for decades, if not centuries. With Börte, Chinggis Khan had four sons and five daughters: Qojin (1179 or 1180), Jochi (1182), Chaghatai (1183 or 1184), Ögödei (1186), Checheyigen (1187 or 1188), Alaqa (1189 or 1190), Tümelün (1192), Tolui (1194), and Al Altan (1196). (Broadbridge, 67) This section will focus on Chinggis Khan's relationship with his sons due to the paucity of information concerning his daughters. Indeed, the section in *The Secret History* which would discuss his daughters appears to have been redacted. (SHM, §215) While he also had other offspring with his other wives, the children from Börte, his first and senior wife, would rule the empire.

Jochi was born in the camp of Jamuqa not long after Temüjin rescued Börte with the aid of Jamuqa and Toghril. Due to the timing of the birth, the *Secret History of the Mongols* hints that Jochi's father may have been a Merkit rather than Temüjin. One must keep in mind that several months passed before Börte's rescue. Although Temüjin always viewed Jochi as the eldest son, others, such as Chaghadai, did not. The Persian sources, including Rashid al-Din, who had access to Mongol documents like the *Shengwu qinzheng lu*, as well as senior Mongol officials not only from the Ilkhanid court in Persia but also those who had served in the court of Khubilai Khan, never mentioned Jochi's questionable lineage. Of anyone, it should have been Rashid al-Din, as the heirs of Jochi were a considerable thorn in the side of his patrons in the Ilkhanate.

Despite his father's recognition and regardless of whether Jochi was a Merkit bastard, there were clear tensions. It is doubtful that they were due to any expectation of being Chinggis Khan's successor. Succession was never based on primogeniture or ultimogeniture among the Mongols. Rather, it was decided in a *quriltai*, based ideally on the principle of the best-qualified relative of Chinggis Khan. Thus, the successor could be the eldest, the youngest, or even a lateral successor, should none of the sons be suitable. Tensions did not arise immediately, and Temüjin seemingly showed Jochi all proper respect. Jochi helped to extend Mongol authority into Siberia by bringing the Hoyin Irgen under Mongol control in 1207-1209. He also accompanied Sübedei in pursuing the fleeing Merkit to the steppes north of the Aral Sea, where the Merkit took refuge with Qangli nomads. In addition to destroying the Merkit and their Qangli protectors, Jochi and Sübedei fought Muhammad Khwarazmshah in a battle the Mongols did not seek. Although they withdrew under the cover of night, their ferocity left Sultan Muhammad shaken and more than a bit concerned about the Mongols. Jochi also took part in the wars against the Jin Empire. Accompanied by his brothers Ögödei and Chaghadai, he captured the stud pastures of the Jin, a grievous blow that certainly hindered the Jin's ability to replace horses. During the Khwarazmian war, Jochi received an independent command that swept west from Otrar and captured the cities along the Syr Darya River while he advanced on the Khwarazmian capital of Urgench.

Chaghadai and Ögödei soon joined him. Jochi took his time in attacking Urgench, as it would fall into the territory allotted to him. Thus, he wanted to mitigate the damage to this trade city. Unfortunately, its resistance frustrated the Mongols, causing Chaghadai and Ögödei to grow impatient. They advocated a more aggressive approach to the siege. This led to a round of finger-pointing on all sides and further delayed the siege. When the city finally fell, the three brothers divided the pillage among them, but neglected to send a share of it to their father. There were several occasions when Chinggis Khan became angry in *The Secret History of the Mongols*. This was one of them. His anger was not due to avarice, but rather insubordination. From his position as Chinggis Khan, all plunder was his by right. This did not mean that he kept it, but he would redistribute it. Of course, those at the scene of the victory also had a claim to the loot, but only a portion of it. As with previous occasions, Chinggis Khan's advisors had to restrain him from severely punishing his sons. Bo'orchu and Shiqi Qutuqu reminded him that his sons were young and still learning the ways of war. (SHM, §260)

As the Mongols withdrew from the Khwarazmian Empire, Jochi remained in the steppes of modern Kazakhstan. The region north of the Aral Sea and Lake Balkhash became part of his patrimony. He had the additional task of bringing any Turkic tribes in the vicinity under Mongol sway. This also fell into the scope of another mission, to assist Sübedei on his return from his reconnaissance mission. Jochi's help was much needed because Sübedei faced continual harassment from Kipchak tribes and troops from the merchant city of Bulgar on the Volga River. Without Jochi's army to provide relief, it is unlikely that Sübedei could have completed his mission.

When Chinggis Khan returned to Mongolia to prepare for the campaign of retribution against Xi Xia, Jochi did not join him. He remained in the steppes, securing the region of the Volga River and hunting—his favorite activity. Although Jochi had proven to be an adept commander, his real passion was hunting, which the sources emphasize over his military capacity. Jochi died in 1225, leaving several wives and, according to one source, 40 sons, although less than 20 were known by name. (JT, 246) His heirs would conquer territories from the Volga River to the Carpathian Mountains and invade Central Europe.

It is rumored that Jochi ignored Chinggis Khan's order for him to join in the final Xi Xia campaign. Sübedei went directly from Jochi's camp to lead the vanguard against Xi Xia, while Jochi remained in the steppes. His absence and increasing independence annoyed Chinggis Khan. Although Chinggis Khan only granted Jochi 9000 people for his patrimony, as the Mongol Empire expanded, the Jochids never lacked troops because of the numerous Turkic tribes in a territory that stretched from the Irtysh River to the Volga River at the time of Jochi's death.

Chaghadai was the second eldest son and an ardent opponent of Jochi. While on campaign, he and Jochi quarreled over who would be the successor. It was not so much about who would be the heir, but whether Jochi could even be considered. Chaghadai was adamant that he would never listen to the Merkit bastard. Not only did they brawl, but they did so in court and in front of their father. Needless to say, Chaghadai did not impress Chinggis Khan with his leadership abilities either.

As portrayed in the sources, Chaghadai viewed the world in Manichaean terms. He was obstinate in his outlook, which clearly affected his ability as a ruler and leader. Yet, his loyalty, once given, was unstinting. In most campaigns, he paired with his slightly younger brother Ögödei, who may have balanced Chaghadai's stubborn streak with his own more relaxed manner. Although Chaghadai experienced success in warfare, he was not known for his military career. While he may have been stalwart in his views, he truly embraced his father's vision and became the prime adherent of the *yasa* and *yosin*, or laws and customs of Chinggis Khan. For him, his father was the paradigm of virtue, whose example all should follow. From the sources, one gets the sense that Chaghadai did and part of his punctilious interpretation was because of his own inability to emulate his father in other areas. Chinggis Khan bequeathed Chaghadai 8000 people and an appanage that included Mawarannahr and into modern Xinjiang.

Ögödei, Chinggis Khan's third son, appears early in history. He suffered a grievous neck wound during the battle against the Kereit in 1203, when he was roughly 17 years old. As previously mentioned, Boroqul rescued Ögödei and cared for him during their retreat to Lake Baljuna. Without Boroqul, Ögödei surely would have died. It is perhaps due to this near-death experience that Ögödei appears as more light-hearted—although also prone to anger and seriousness—than his brothers. Yet, he could also be petty, grousing about his commanders while he was a mediocre general at best. What marked him as different from the rest of his brothers was that while he did not excel as a military leader or warrior, he was likable and able to get others to work together. As already mentioned, Jochi, Chaghadai, and Ögödei led a few armies together. Considering the rivalry between Jochi and Chaghadai, it is difficult to believe they could have been successful without Ögödei's presence acting as a buffer and a mediator between the two princes.

Chinggis Khan allotted Ögödei an appanage that included western Mongolia and stretched to the Tian Shan Mountains, while also providing him 5000 people. Although his army was smaller than his elder brothers', Ögödei eventually became Chinggis Khan's successor. He was named the heir at the brawl between Jochi and Chaghadai, but this status was not guaranteed. Indeed, it simply meant that Chinggis Khan preferred Ögödei—it did not mean that the *quriltai* had to select him. It did, however, particularly as Chinggis Khan's word became almost sacred and inviolable. Despite his more easy-going manner, Ögödei had much of his father in him. He lacked the rigid world view of Chaghadai and was flexible in his views, although his pride sometimes blinded his vision and he loved his wine. He also continued with his father's expectations. Just as Chinggis Khan trusted his commanders but recognized their limitations in controlling his sons and other relatives, so did Ögödei. When his own son Güyük disparaged Jochi's son Batu during the campaign that conquered Russia, Güyük was sent to his father. Ögödei's wrath matched Chinggis Khan's in pouring derision upon his son. Indeed, only Ögödei's untimely death prevented Güyük from being sent to fight on the front lines of the Song Empire—not as a commander, but as a common soldier. Like his father, Ögödei expected unity among the *altan urugh*.

Chinggis Khan's youngest son, Tolui, may have been his most capable. As a child, he narrowly escaped being killed by a Tatar slave. Despite his youth, he led armies in the Jin war, albeit under the tutelage of trusted commanders. His coming-out party, so to speak, was the Khwarazmian war, where he led a campaign of destruction in Khurasan, a territory now divided between Iran, Afghanistan, and Turkmenistan. After Chinggis Khan's death, Tolui became the regent and handled the affairs of the empire until his brother Ögödei took the throne. There was a moment when it was feasible for Tolui to assume the throne, but his father's words took on almost sacred qualities, thus preventing other candidates from being considered as his successor. He inherited the pastures of his father as well as 5000 people. Of course, by gaining his father's pastures, he acquired most of Mongolia as well. Although he died relatively young in 1232, his children from Sorqoqtani (Möngke, Qubilai, Hülegü, and Ariq-Böke) shaped the future of the Mongol Empire.

7. The Art of War

Outside of Chinggis Khan's *ger* stood his *tuq*. This standard or banner was made with nine horse or yak tails. Normally in time of peace, the tails hanging from it were white, but occasionally, another *tuq* stood in its place with black tails swaying in the breeze to indicate war. Considering the Mongol conquests, one can wonder which saw the light of day the most.

Chinggis Khan not only unified the steppes, but he also dramatically transformed steppe warfare and indeed warfare in general. While calling his military reforms revolutionary might be too strong, Chinggis Khan undoubtedly transformed steppe warfare into a more refined military system. This was a substantial change in itself as nomadic horse-archers had become the most dominant element on the battlefield since the Scythian era. Although Roman legions and armored knights attract the most attention in the popular mind, few things were more terrifying in the pre-modern world than seeing bands of bow-wielding riders on their shaggy horses on the horizon.

The terror this image evoked was not just due to the Mongols' accuracy with arrows, but also the fact that the nomads were mobile and fast. While other horses might be faster than those the nomads rode, few, if any, had better endurance or were tougher. The horses of Mongolia could survive the sub-arctic temperatures of winter, dig through snow and ice to find grass, and gallop for miles. That the nomads had thousands of horses made them even more dangerous, as they would switch mounts so as not to exhaust their horses. This also allowed them to cover more ground when they desired. Until mechanized warfare, the average army traveled up to an astounding 20-25 miles a day. Even today, 25 miles is still considered good progress for a large army. Typically, the Mongols traveled with their families as well as flocks and herds. As anyone who has dealt with sheep can tell you, long-distance travel is not their forte. Yet, when the Mongols needed to, their armies could cover 100 miles or more in a single day by swapping horses. On average, the Mongol soldier took five horses with him on campaign and avoided riding the same horse consecutively to always keep their mounts fresh.

Mongol warfare was more than just nomads prowling around the steppes. Since time immemorial, nomadic archers had been deadly because of their ability to shower their opponents with arrows while keeping out of reach of the enemy, occasionally turning in the saddle and shooting arrows as they retreated. The most common tactic was a feigned retreat in which the nomads goaded the enemy into charging them. The nomads then rode away with their enemy in pursuit, close but not within reach. The nomads lured their enemy into an ambush point or tempted them so that their forces became drawn out and no longer in formation. At this point, the nomads turned and eliminated the disorganized enemy. Additionally, they were successful in encircling maneuvers so that their troops would suddenly strike at the flanks or the rear of the enemy. Surrounded, the nomads then used archery to eliminate the pinned-down enemy. They succeeded because their composite bows were frequently superior to those of their sedentary enemies, and also virtually all the nomads were archers. Due to its range, power, utility in hunting, and that it was easier to make than a sword—which required a blacksmith—the bow was the supreme weapon on the steppe. While blacksmiths existed on the steppes, they were not common. Of course, high-quality bows required specialization and not all nomads were skilled bowyers, so the latter became highly valued artisans.

Yet, these Central Eurasian nomads all fought in very similar ways, whether they were Kipchaks near the Black Sea, the Qarluqs in modern Kazakhstan, or Tatars in eastern Mongolia. So what did Chinggis Khan do to separate his army from the others? Considering that his fortunes in war improved after he returned from his decade-long absence in the Jin Empire, he apparently learned more about tactics and strategies. Some of his adjustments were simple, such as forbidding his men from engaging in plundering the enemy before victory was secured. Too many battles could be lost if men sought to increase their economic status while the fighting went on. Brilliant tacticians such as Salah al-Din (Saladin) in the Crusades and even divinely guided leaders like the Prophet Muhammad lost battles because of the lack of discipline among their armies. One should not blame the average warrior for being tempted by a nice piece of jewelry he spotted while killing the inhabitants of a tent. Additionally, the shares of loot usually worked on a pyramid level with the higher-ups getting more. Chinggis Khan changed this and ensured a more fair distribution of loot. Undoubtedly, he was influenced by the poverty of his childhood. Although he came from an aristocratic family, he also understood deprivation. Again, this was not a revolutionary innovation. Many commanders in the steppes, as well as among sedentary armies, had stressed the need for discipline among the rank and file to prevent the enemy from rallying.

Nonetheless, it was a transformative moment, as the emphasis on discipline laid the foundation for more profound innovations. One of them was the introduction of a decimal organization based on units of 10, 100, and 1000. Again, it was not a radical change, as decimal units had been in use since the Xiongnu period (200 BCE-200 CE) and had continued to be practiced into the Liao Empire (965-1125) that dominated most of Mongolia. Indeed, the Khitans still used them during Chinggis Khan's early career as Toghril's *nökör*. However, Chinggis Khan took this system to new levels as he gradually organized society around this concept, so that his new empire was geared for war. Households, in a particular *minggan* (unit of 1000) supported the military *minggan*. Furthermore, as the *minggan* was based on 10 *jaghuns* (units of 100), he only needed to give commands to 10 subordinates, who then gave commands to their 10 subordinates, the commanders of the 10 *arbans* (a squad of 10) that formed a *jaghun*. Thus, command structures were streamlined. While not every unit was always at full strength, it also provided the commanders a quick estimate of how many men they had and could assign units across the battlefield relatively easily.

Furthermore, it was expected that a commander of an *arban* could assume command of a larger unit if necessary. Thus, the death of a commander on the battlefield did not mean ruin. In essence, commanders, while valued, were not viewed as irreplaceable. Napoleon would later commit to the idea that all of his soldiers should carry a marshal's baton in their backpacks, although it seems unlikely that he adopted the idea from Chinggis Khan.

The battle of Chakirma'ut

With discipline and a flexible command structure, Chinggis Khan could now venture away from the standard steppe tactics of encirclements, feigned retreats, and flanking maneuvers. His new formations and tactics were unveiled at the battle of Chakirma'ut in 1204. While the Mongols fought the Naiman, others who sought to resist Chinggis Khan's new order on the steppe joined them. In *The Secret History of the Mongols*, Jamuqa serves as the play-by-play announcer for Tayang Khan. Although it seems unlikely that the narration took place as depicted, the scene provides us with important information about the battle, namely that the Mongols used tactics and formations previously unseen on the steppes. In the prelude to the battle, we see a number of changes.

The Mongols approached the battle by disguising their numbers and conditions. They allowed some of their horses to run loose so the Naiman could capture them. These horses were skinny and in poor shape, as the battle took place in early spring before they had fattened up from the winter. The Mongols made a determined march to catch the Naiman off guard. While their arrival was not a complete surprise, the Mongols also attempted to lull the Naiman into a false sense of security by revealing the weakened condition of their mounts—an aspect that any nomad would appreciate. The Mongols disguised their numbers also by lighting many campfires at night, making their camp appear much larger than reality.

The Art of War | 101

Throughout their campaigns, the Mongols used similar tricks such as tying branches to their horses' tails in order to create a larger dust cloud or putting dummies on their spare horses so a distant observer saw an army that again exceeded reality. They could combine this tactic with having the horses led over a ridge in single file to mask the size of their units. Considering that each warrior had five horses, the Mongols might display an army of overwhelming strength, thus undermining the morale of the enemy even before the battle began.

Yet, this subterfuge was simply a preamble to battle. The Mongol marched to the Chakirma'ut in *qaraghana* or bush formation, meaning in small groups. While the precise meaning is not clear, the impression is that they marched in a spread-out formation probably to prevent surprise attacks as they entered Naiman territory. Also, being spread out would not prevent them from unifying against an attack. In short, the *qaraghana* formation permitted the Mongols to have flexibility as they marched and the ability to deal with any threats.

When they arrived at the battle site, Chinggis Khan arrayed the army into "*na'ur*" or lake formation. This gave them a wide formation with depth. Here, it was especially important because the Naiman outnumbered the Mongols. By using the *na'ur*, however, the Mongols could then overlap the Naiman armies. As the Naiman were positioned on the high ground on a mountain slope, the Mongols thus denied them room to deploy their full force. This also demonstrated the Mongols' preference to fight at a location of their own choosing. If they found the enemy's location unfavorable, the Mongols then attempted to lure them to a more suitable site with feigned retreats and other efforts at subterfuge. At the Battle of the Kalka River, for instance, the Mongol vanguard lured the combined Kipchak and Rus' force for nine days across the steppe to an ambush location favorable to the Mongols.

While the *na'ur* was a formation for deployment, the Mongols then engaged the enemy by using a *shi'uchi*, or chisel tactic, continually attacking the enemy. For the Mongols, this meant that from the *na'ur* their armies were in files, most likely composed of single *arbans*. Across the lakefront, so to speak, the files would ride forth and shoot arrows, then circle back to provide a continuous attack. In doing so, the riders could shoot as they approached and then retreat. At the same time, the Mongols did not come near enough for close combat or get into a medley so that the enemy could time a counter-attack. For the Naiman at Chakirma'ut, to surge forward, risked exposing their ranks for flanking or rear attack by the Mongols. The attack with archery from this base formation could also suddenly change to a charge with lance or sabre, or if the enemy did charge, the Mongols could then retreat in good order while also shooting the enemy and potentially luring them into an ambush. Furthermore, from this position, the Mongols could cease with the *shi'uchi* tactic and switch to another tactic such as an arrow storm, which meant shooting their arrows at designated kill zones. The idea was not targeting individuals but an area with a barrage, so that the enemy indiscriminately endured a rain of arrows. The Mongol commanders signaled their intent through whistling arrows or the use of flags, thus controlling their armies even in the din of battle. Thus, it was preferable for the army commander not to lead from the front, but to direct the battle from a vantage point where he could observe not only his own forces, but also how the enemy deployed their units.

While the Battle of Chakirma'ut revealed new wrinkles in the fabric of steppe warfare, the Mongols continued to refine their art of war. Chinggis Khan focused on the destruction of the enemy, particularly their command structure, as a paramount goal. In doing so, as he did in the Khwarazmian campaign, he assigned specific task forces to hunt the enemy commander once the opportunity arose. This prevented the adversary leader from rallying his forces. Furthermore, the sight of a fleeing ruler or commander must have also affected the morale of his armies. With no time to recover, the Mongols also kept the advantage, forcing the enemy to respond to Mongol actions rather than initiating their own plans.

While most of the Mongol forces, particularly in Chinggis Khan's lifetime, were nomadic horse archers, the Mongols also created armies of sedentary forces, both cavalry and infantry. Nomads were incorporated into the Mongol military system; if conquered, they were distributed among the existing units and given a Mongol haircut, much like one gets a new haircut when joining the modern military. The idea was to establish a new identity—a Mongol one. Furthermore, the distinctive haircut, which was a tonsure like a monk's, but leaving a tuft of hair in the front, and allowing the back to grow long and be braided, lessened the chance of desertion, as it made one easily identifiable. Sedentary troops, however, retained their own identities and were not forced to conform to the Mongol style of fighting, although there are some indications they had to adopt the Mongol haircut. There was no sense in putting square pegs in round holes. The Mongols used these where needed. Furthermore, any part of a submission agreement included providing troops to the Mongols when requested. Failure to do so was viewed as an act of rebellion. Additionally, non-Mongol commanders were not limited. Above all, Chinggis Khan valued ability and thus non-Mongol commanders could even command Mongol units once they demonstrated their talent. More frequently, however, they often acted with Mongol commanders, as there was a level of difficulty in transitioning from commanding units of infantry to the highly mobile Mongol cavalry.

Although the Mongols were novices at siege warfare, they quickly adapted to new technologies and sought expertise. A corps of siege engineers also came into being. Mongol tactics at siege warfare varied with the size and defenses of a location. Often, the Mongols simply stormed it when possible. Rather than surrounding a large city, they typically blockaded it with mobile units who could intercept relief forces while also keeping foraging parties and sorties from the city or fortress confined. At smaller locations, it was not uncommon for the Mongols to build a palisade around the city, which not only provided the Mongols with defenses, but also helped keep the defenders confined. The Mongols did not build walls themselves, but impressed the local population and then herded them to the desired location. Thus, the besieged defenders had to kill their own people. Additionally, the "arrow fodder" also carried rubble and other debris to fill any moats of defensive ditches. Once a clear path to the walls existed, the "arrow fodder" then attempted to breach the walls with battering rams, thus sparing the Mongols from the riskiest part of the sieges. Once they breached the wall, however, the Mongols did the fighting. The Mongols also scaled the walls with a simple ladder, although the Mongols soon incorporated "cloud ladders" from China. These were on a mobile platform, some of which also offered a modicum of protection.

Once familiar with siege engines, the Mongols could amass larger numbers before a stronghold. While the Mongols' siege train included equipment broken down and transported on camels to be reassembled on-site, the Mongols were not averse to building their own equipment (under the guidance of engineers) *in situ*. This could take time, however. The Mongols gradually refined their techniques and massed their artillery at specific points to reduce walls quickly. In 1260, the Mongol armies reduced the vaunted defenses of Aleppo in Syria, in five days. Remember the armies of the Crusades and the Byzantine Empire failed to achieve this even before the Aleppan defenses were improved during the Ayyubid period (1171-1260).

The Mongol military under Chinggis Khan became an incredible and devastating force capable of unleashing almost Armageddon-like destruction upon its opponents. The only thing that may have exceeded it was its reputation. Like most armies, the Mongols engaged in psychological warfare to enhance their reputation. They continue to have a reputation that places them on a par with, or perhaps worse than, the anti-Christ or mythological creatures, such as Gog and Magog, whose presence signaled the end of time. Today, scientists believe that the destruction caused by the Mongols may have actually lowered carbon levels based on the number of people killed. While a modern reader may be horrified by these descriptions and some modern scholars have downplayed the level of destruction wrought by the Mongols, I suspect that Chinggis Khan himself would be pleased with his legacy of brutality. This is exactly what he wished for. The Mongols wanted people to believe the worst of them, as fear was their ally. Once word reached enough people that the Mongols destroyed all who opposed them, they quickly gained the submission of many cities without even fighting. Those that submitted found themselves left alone, as long as they abided by the terms of surrender: provide troops, provisions, pay tribute, and the ruler needed to submit formally to the Mongol leader in due course. Failure to do so was an invitation to destruction.

8. The Wit and Wisdom of Chinggis Khan

After Chinggis Khan's death, his empire did not fragment as so many others, created through rapid conquest by strong-willed individuals like Alexander the Great, Tamerlane, and Napoleon did. Chinggis Khan suffered only two major defeats in 40 years. In both cases, he apparently came back stronger than before. The first was when Jamuqa defeated him in 1187. The second was death in 1227. Yet, even death could not truly stop him. His influence and legacy continued far beyond the grave. Indeed, perhaps in death, Chinggis Khan became even more powerful and influential. He ceased to be a mortal and, in effect, became a demi-god.

Much of this transformation has to do with the indigenous religious beliefs of the medieval Mongols. In the Mongolian culture of that era, the afterlife was not transcendental. One did not go to the equivalent of heaven or paradise. One simply became a spirit and lived a life in the spirit world equivalent to one's life in the mundane. Thus, if you were a common nomad, you lived with your flocks and herds for all eternity. Occasionally, your relatives would make offerings to you. Overall, not a bad (after)life. A khan, however, lived a life similar to the one in the earthly realm. You had better food and drink than a nomad and, of course, more stuff: nicer horses, women, riches, etc. Your spiritual power was greater too and was appropriate to your stature. This is one reason the Naiman queen, Gürbesü, took Toghril's skull and offered sacrifices to it. First, she wanted to propitiate Toghril, so he did not seek spiritual revenge against the Naiman after a scout failed to recognize the Kereit khan and killed him. Secondly, Toghril had been a powerful figure. If she could tap into that power, then the veneration was beneficial.

Now, consider the case of Chinggis Khan. Even in our modern and jaded world, he still continues to amaze people. Historically, no other ruler had conquered more territory. On a comparative scale, it could be argued that no other ruler had been as destructive either. While the Jin Empire survived him, it was a fragment of its former self and only held its own against a portion of his army. Indeed, when he departed on the Khwarazmian campaign, Chinggis Khan's actions indicated he no longer viewed the Jin Empire as a serious threat. Additionally, Chinggis Khan unified all the tribes of Mongolia, destroying the power of not only the Jin Empire, but also erasing the Khwarazmian Empire (the largest Islamic state at the time), Xi Xia, and Qara Khitai from the map. One could argue that Güchülüg had effectively usurped the Qara Khitai throne in 1211, but in reality, he did not seek to create a new kingdom, but simply rule the existing Qara Khitai state. Chinggis Khan's achievements dwarfed anyone else's in both the 12th and 13th centuries. Furthermore, his sons continued to expand the empire until it stretched from the Balkan Mountains to the Sea of Japan, making it the largest contiguous empire in history. One must consider the following question: just how much spiritual power must Chinggis Khan have possessed once in the spirit world?

His accomplishments elevated much of his deeds and words into an inviolable status. After Chinggis Khan died, his body was transported and entombed. Exactly where is unknown. Allegedly, the escort killed all whom they encountered and Chinggis Khan was buried on the slopes of Mount Burqan Qaldun, a holy site where he had to take refuge on more than one occasion in his youth. Another legend is that the cart carrying his remains became stuck while returning from Xi Xia. As a result, the Mongols buried him in what is now Inner Mongolia. Indeed, one group of Mongols claims to be the descendants of the guards who remained to protect the tomb. Of course, if guards were being left, then killing everyone they encountered does not make much sense, as they were not exactly hidden. On the other hand, the legend certainly enhanced the sacral nature of Chinggis Khan's new life after death.

Several expeditions have sought to find Chinggis Khan's tomb and all of them have failed. In the 1990s, a Japanese team used ground-penetrating radar to search for the tomb without success. They did, however, identify other potential gravesites and thus benefitted from the archaeological study of Mongolia. In the late 1990s and early 2000s, a Chicago stock trader, Maury Kravitz, claimed he knew the tomb's location and financed a couple of expeditions. Those failed as well. In all likelihood, the tomb has already been found but kept secret or will not be found, in part because there are those who have no interest in disturbing Chinggis Khan's eternal rest.

Yet, Chinggis Khan lived on in word and deed. His decrees became encapsulated in the *Yasa*, the laws of the Mongol Empire. This was a combination of custom and Chinggis Khan's decrees. His successors would add to the body of work. Unfortunately, what the *Yasa* was remains unclear as a formal copy or codification never took place or, at least, survived. Indeed, it was rumored that only the ruling family actually had access to the *Yasa*, which seems an odd way to rule an empire. Then again, the *altan urugh* viewed the Mongol Empire more as a family enterprise, so the *Yasa* may have simply been based on their consensus and decisions. We know it did not supplant local laws even though it did override them when disputes arose.

What follows are a series of quotes and actions from Chinggis Khan which reveal much of his personality and character. Some may be apocryphal but they come from *The Secret History of the Mongols* and Rashid al-Din's *Jami' al-tawarikh* (The Compendium of Chronicles).

Generosity, loyalty, unity

When rustlers stole Chinggis Khan's family's horses in his youth, he pursued them. Bo'orchu joined him, and the interaction between the two revealed much about the young Temüjin's outlook. When they were pursued after recovering their horses, only Temüjin had a bow.

Bo'orchu insisted on covering their escape. The young Temüjin said, "I do not want you hurt for my sake. I will exchange arrows with him!" (SHM §91) Then, after they reached safety, Temüjin said, "My friend, without you, I could never have recovered these horses. Let us divide them. Tell me how many you will take." (SHM §92) This episode tells us two things about Chinggis Khan's character. The first is that he appreciated Bo'orchu's unexpected friendship and assistance. Secondly, he would not expect or accept someone else to take unnecessary risks on his behalf. Finally, it also demonstrates his generosity. Temüjin's family only had a few horses, yet he was willing to give his newfound friend a portion of those horses out of loyalty and gratitude. Although Bo'orchu refused (his father was wealthy anyway), that Temüjin made the gesture endeared him to Bo'orchu. Similar circumstances also arose with others, but through this incident with Bo'orchu, one can see how Temüjin's charisma drew people into his service.

Bo'orchu appears in another discussion regarding loyalty. After he became khan of the Borjigid Mongols, Temüjin turned to Bo'orchu and Jelme (who had been given to him as a servant) and said:

> When, apart from my shadow, I had no friends,
>   you were my shadows.
> You eased my mind,
> So in my mind you shall stay.
> When, apart from my tail, I had no fat,
> You were my tail.
> You eased my heart,
> So in my breast you shall stay. (SHM §125)

In this passage, a few items are revealed. The first is that Temüjin refers to the days of his youth, when his family was indigent. The reference to no friends but his own shadow refers to the abandonment of his family by the former followers of Yesügei. The reference to no fat apart from his tail is an allusion to the tail of a sheep. Mutton served as the primary food for the Mongols. Sheep in Mongolia have a fat tail and is kept on the sheep, unlike in the

United States, which is docked or cut off while young, so that urine and dung do not build on the tail and attract flies, leading to health hazards for the sheep. The Mongolian sheep are not as selectively bred (particularly in Temüjin's time) so they can lift their tail (and survive in a harsher climate). The fat also refers to prosperity. The phrase "fat and happy" is quite appropriate for nomads, as it provides a context about how their animals are doing. If the animals are fat (as indicated by the condition of the sheep's tail), then there is good pasture; if the animals are doing well, then the nomad's overall condition is good. Temüjin's statement thus indicates that Bo'orchu and Jelme stayed with him even when he did not experience success. Moreover, they eased his worries and for that, he would always love and appreciate them for their deeds, which also indicates that Chinggis Khan possessed a good barometer for judging the character of his companions.

Prompted by his wife Yisui Khatun, Chinggis Khan thought about which of his sons would succeed him, as neither primogeniture nor ultimogeniture served as the primary forms of succession among the Mongols. When Chinggis Khan asked Jochi what were his thoughts, Chaghadai interrupted and asked "How could we be governed by a bastard of the Merkits?" Jochi's response was to grab Chaghadai and ask him why he belittled him when their father does not and asked him why he considers himself superior, when "Only in terms of stupidity are you perhaps superior." (SHM, §254). The two then engaged in fisticuffs and had to be separated. After tempers calmed, Chinggis Khan continued with his evaluation of his sons. Ultimately, Ögödei was chosen, partially because everyone could agree on him. He also chided Jochi and Chaghadai,

> Do not let people laugh at you,
> do not let others ridicule you (SHM, §255).

In this episode, Chinggis Khan recognized the personalities of his sons, but reminded them that if their rivalry and disagreements became a source of dissension, it would harm their overall reputation. Concerned about perception, Chinggis Khan wanted unity in his family. In his chastisement of his sons, he reminded them how Altan and Quchar betrayed him. Undoubtedly, he also reflected on the trials and tribulations of his youth, when his family had been abandoned by his uncles and other relatives. Ultimately, this exchange tells us that he realized how fragile his new empire was and that if his heirs did not maintain unity, it could easily fall apart. The themes of unity and legacy are reflected in Rashid al-Din's *Jami'at al-tawarikh* or *Compendium of Chronicles*, one of the first systematic attempts at world history written in the early 14th century and commissioned by Chinggis Khan's descendants in Persia.

One section includes parables and examples of Chinggis Khan's wisdom and character. The first example focuses on the longevity of the empire. "Among my offspring, many emperors will come into existence after this. If the grandees and warriors who will serve them do not maintain the *yasaq* (sic) strictly, the empire will become shaky and end. They will wish they had [Chinggis] Khan, but they will not have him." (JT, 201)

The message is clear. While the previous example addressed his offspring, this passage discusses those who served the Mongols. He recognized that his commanders and others in high positions always needed to focus on the empire. The emphasis on the *Yasa* or *yasaq*, as it entered the Persian sources, is clear. The *Yasa* maintained the integrity of the empire in Chinggis Khan's view. It was not enough for only the rulers to abide by it, but all members of the elite as well. The final mention of wanting another Chinggis Khan is not just a moment of vainglory, but also a reference to wishing for a leader of Chinggis Khan's stature and values. In other words, the rulers needed to promote the integrity of the state and ensure that commanders and grandees do not take advantage of their positions and become complacent by circumventing the laws of the empire and holding themselves above it. Even if the quotes were apocryphal (a possibility we cannot rule out), Chinggis Khan's status provided him the gravitas to be the exemplar of morality and wisdom for the Mongols, particularly for the *altan urugh*.

Another example of matters of state is made through a discussion of horses. "A horse that runs well when it is fat, when it is half-fleshed, and when it is lean can be called a good horse. A horse that runs well in only one of these three conditions cannot be called good." (JT 201) The intent is obvious—one must consider the quality of a ruler, state, or anything not only when it is in the best of condition, but even when they are at their weakest.

"No word spoken that is true, whether spoken in seriousness or in jest, can ever be taken back." (JT, 202) One can only take a moment to wonder what Chinggis Khan would think of social media. His wisdom here cannot be disputed, as everyone has had thoughts better left unsaid. I suspect Chinggis Khan would not be a fan of Twitter.

"There is no warrior like [Yisügei] Bahadur, and no one else possesses the skills he had, but he did not suffer from hardship and was not affected by hunger or thirst. He thought his liege men could tolerate hardship as well as he could, but they couldn't. A man is worthy of leadership who knows what hunger and thirst are and who can judge the condition of others thereby, who can go at a measured pace and not allow the soldiers to get hungry and thirsty or the horse to get worn out. The proverb 'Travel the pace of the weakest among you' is an allusion to this." (JT, 202) His wisdom here is one that all leaders should heed. The proverb mentioned is excellent advice derived from the life of a nomad. If one travels faster than the weakest animals, then the flocks and herds quickly diminish. The same will be true in other cases. His point about the warrior Yisügai (not his father) is valid. While it is good to push others so they strive to meet their potential, one must understand the limits that individuals have. A good leader will understand this, a poor leader will not, and view lesser abilities as weakness, thus breaking the individual.

"After us, our offspring will wear gold-brocaded robes and eat sweet and fatty tidbits. They will ride beautiful horses and embrace lovely ladies. They will not say, 'These things were assembled by our fathers and elders'. On that day of greatness they will forget us." (JT,

203) In this quote, we have Chinggis Khan, perhaps on his deathbed, contemplating his life and legacy. Considering his achievements, his wistful statement is one that probably many have thought. It is a reflection on the fact that the status of many is often due to the success of those who came before and not their own abilities.

One day Chinggis Khan asked a number of his companions, "What is best in life?" A number of his companions responded in some variation that hunting with falcons on the open steppe was best. Chinggis Khan responded, "You have all spoken well, but a man's greatest pleasure is to defeat his enemies, to uproot them, to take what they have, to make their women weep so that tears run down their noses, to mount their fair-gaited, fat-thighed stallions, and to clothe the bellies and navels of beautiful ladies with thin nightclothes and to look at and kiss their rouged cheeks, and to suck their sweet, ruby-colored lips." (JT, 206)

This was later paraphrased in the 1982 movie *Conan*. Where a Hyrkanian khan (clearly modeled after the Mongols as Conan's creator, Robert E. Howard, intended), after learning his armies won another victory, asks his assembled commanders, "This is good, but what is best in life?" one of his commanders proudly gives the hunting response. The khan then turns to the stern Conan, who replies, "Crush your enemies, see them driven before them and hear the lamentation of their women." The movie paraphrasing of the Chinggis Khan quote has more appeal, but also omits some of his thought. Chinggis Khan enjoyed hunting, as most Mongol men did, but he also appreciated riding horses and the company of women. Considering the number of wives and concubines he had, this should come as no surprise. Yet of equal importance is his emphasis on crushing his enemies. Chinggis Khan took pleasure in battle and victory. There should be no confusion on this. If he went to war reluctantly, he did not fight so. He fought to win and win decisively so that his enemies could never trouble him again.

While there are many other aphorisms and anecdotes from the life of Chinggis Khan, what do these tell us about his character? He truly lived a rags-to-riches life, but I doubt he would ever claim to be a self-made man, as he recognized the contributions of others and handsomely rewarded them for it. While Chinggis Khan was an amazing leader, much of his leadership ability stemmed from learning the lessons from his mistakes, as well as choosing the right people. Early on, little indicated that Temüjin would become Chinggis Khan, yet he still attracted people of talent, such as Bo'orchu. However, when he separated from Jamuqa, he found himself thrust into a position of great leadership. This occurred in part because his elders sought to use him, but at the same time, several other people also joined him because they preferred Temüjin's leadership style and innate charisma over that of the more experienced, but arrogant Jamuqa. His assortment of experiences and the lessons he learned taught him how to relate to people and appreciate their abilities and character rather than their family name or social status.

As mentioned, Chinggis Khan possessed a quick temper, but one that he learned to master. As he matured, he waited until he calmed down before making rash decisions. In recognizing his faults, Chinggis Khan surrounded himself with trusted advisors, ranging from his mother and wives to close companions. All of them could speak freely and warn him of the consequences of impulsive decisions. He valued their wisdom. Furthermore, he listened to criticism and learned from it, even if he did not accept it gracefully. While his word was law, Chinggis Khan's pride did not interfere with decisions. He sought and was willing to hear different views, as demonstrated by his experiences with religious holy men. The latter experiences also show a fascination with his legacy. While he sought immortality or at least a longer life, there can be little doubt that Chinggis Khan wanted to be remembered.

9. Chinggis vs. Genghis

In most popular publications on the Mongols, whether newspaper articles, novels, general histories, or even the captions in documentaries, one will still see "Genghis" instead of Chinggis. In the west, Chinggis Khan, one of the world's greatest leaders, continually has his name mispronounced. There really is no excuse for it in the English-speaking world. We have all the phonemes to say "Chinggis." So why Genghis? During the reign of the French King Louis XIV (1638-1715), his Arabic and Turkish interpreter, François Pétis, wrote perhaps the first scholarly biography of Chinggis Khan. His son, François Pétis de La Croix, published it in 1710 with the title *Histoire du Grand Genghizcan, Premier Empereur Des Anciens Mogols et Tartares*. From here, Genghis Khan entered the English vocabulary.

The *Historie du Grand Genghizcan* attracted the attention of Penelope Aubin (1679-1731), an English playwright and translator. She translated the book into English and printed it with the London publisher, J. Darby, in 1722. For a title, she simply translated the French without embellishment—*The History of Genghizcan the Great, First Emperor of the Antient Moguls and Tartars*. Before long, the book reached English colonies in North America where none other than Benjamin Franklin helped popularize it through his newspaper. Thomas Jefferson was another proponent of the book. He gave it as gifts and donated a copy to the fledgling Library of Congress, as well as to the library of the University of Virginia, which he founded. As late as 1795, he was in contact with French booksellers seeking more copies.

In French, *Genghiz* has a pronunciation closer to *Jenghiz*, but in English, despite the possibility for a soft "G" like Geoffrey or George, Genghiz became Genghiz with a hard G similar to "gecko". One may ask why François Pétis used "Genghiz" in the first place—a fair question. As an interpreter of Arabic and using Arabic sources within his work, Monsieur Pétis undoubtedly used the Arabic pronunciation in which most Arabic dialects lack a "ch" phoneme. Instead, "ch" would become "zh", "j" as in judge, or when in Egypt, even "g" as in "good". Gradually, Genghizcan transformed into Genghis Khan, with a hard "g" and a correct form of Khan.

It is somewhat surprising that the "Genghizcan" spelling became popular, as the great English historian Edward Gibbon used Zingis Khan in his epic *The Decline and Fall of the Roman Empire* (1776-1789). Whereas few people (including scholars) have read François Pétis' work in the English translation, much less the French, Gibbons' *Decline and Fall* is still considered one of the most important publications in the English language. Still, in the 18th century, both works influenced not only the understanding of history, but also some intellectual ideas, as Jack Weatherford has argued. (Weatherford 2016, xv-xxiii)

Although Weatherford has claimed that Chinggis Khan's attitudes towards religious tolerance influenced Thomas Jefferson and perhaps other American Founding Fathers, the Mongol leader developed another reputation in the 19th and much of the early 20th centuries. While Chinggis Khan's success remained a marvel, too often he became a synonym for barbarity and destruction. To be sure, he still had his admirers, usually scholars who devoted their lives to understanding his accomplishments in the context of his time period. H. H. Howorth wrote a monumental work on the history of not only Chinggis Khan, but also the Mongolian people in general. It remains an unduplicated wonder of 19th-century scholarship. Jeremiah Curtin wrote a history of the Mongols that even merited an introduction by Theodore Roosevelt. Other scholars followed suit.

"Oppressive and regressive force"

Yet while serious scholarship occurred, another view took root. In the mainstream, the concept of "progress," being tied to "taming the land," industrial society, and imperialism—which included rapid military conquest over nomadic and semi-nomadic people across the globe—did much to diminish the fear of the nomadic warriors and their military capability. Pastoral nomadism was viewed as a dead end and barbaric.

This was not localized to Western society. With the rise of Communism, even in Mongolia, Chinggis Khan ceased to be regarded as the founder of the Mongolian people, but simply as a Feudal Horse Lord who oppressed the people. As in the West, there were Mongolian and Soviet scholars who thought otherwise and continued their own work, but quietly, because deviating from party ideology carried great risks. This trend dovetailed nicely with Russian chauvinism and nationalistic history that denied the Mongols conquered the medieval Rus' principalities, while also blaming the Mongols for everything in Russia that might be construed as backwards in comparison with the West. While they slightly modified it during the Soviet era, the theme still held true: Chinggis Khan and the Mongols were an oppressive and regressive force in history.

A good bit of this stemmed from views of the Mongols during the Enlightenment. While Gibbon, Thomas Jefferson, and others obviously believed the Mongols had some merit, even though they deplored their path of destruction, others viewed the Mongols negatively and thought that they contributed little, if anything, of value to humanity. Among these people was the 18th-century French political philosopher, Montesquieu. (Montesquieu, 307)

Thus in the western world, Chinggis Khan transformed into Genghis Khan. While Genghis Khan was in use as his name, the ahistorical view of Chinggis Khan also turned Genghis Khan into a one-dimensional caricature of the Mongol leader. Popular culture reveals much about the prevailing attitudes concerning Chinggis Khan. An excellent starting point is in comic books. Genghis Khan served as a reference to add sudden legitimacy to villains. In Issue 25 of *Aquaman* (1966), the villain is Tamerkhan, a play on Temüjin as well as Tamerlane. Tamerkhan somehow has survived into the 20th century, although he had been in service of Genghis Khan in the 13th century. The connection to Genghis Khan thus provides Tamerkhan instant credibility as a bad guy intent on world domination and other villainy.

Other comparisons are made as well. In *The Incredible Hulk* 4 (1962) comic book, the villain is General Fang, who is called "The most brutal warlord since Ghenghis (sic) Khan." So overt is the inspiration that the title of the story was "Mongu! The Gladiator from Space." The insinuation of Mongols is not subtle.

Genghis Khan was also a popular inspiration for bad behavior. In *The Amazing Spider-Man* 50 (1967), Spider-Man's alter ego, Peter Parker, laments how people view Spider-Man, largely thanks to the negative press given to him by J. Jonah Jameson's *Daily Bugle* newspaper (where Peter worked as a free-lance photographer). Young Parker says, "It's all Jameson's fault! He's got the public convinced that next to me, Genghis Khan was a piker!" Spider-Man's reputation continued to be sullied in 1984 in *Peter Parker, the Spectacular Spider-Man* 9. A couple of delivery men (actually thugs in disguise) ask Spider-Man if he is going to rob them. After Spidey replies that he's a good guy, one of the thugs retorts, "Yeah? Not according to the Daily Bugle, you ain't!" Spidey replies "I know, I know! According to Jolly J. Jonah Jameson's editorials I'm worse than Genghis Khan, Hitler, and Doc Doom all rolled into one! Phooie! I've said it before and I'll say it again—I've just got to get me a good PR man!"

These occurrences were in 1967 and 1984, but the Mongol leader's bad reputation had not been rehabilitated in the popular mind in 2012 either. In Issue 687 of *The Amazing Spider-Man*, Spider-Man's opponent, Dr. Ock (aka. Dr. Octopus) rants, "I shall live on in infamy—a mass murderer worse than Pol Pot, Hitler and Genghis Khan combined." He didn't, thanks to Spider-Man, of course. Marvel Comic's longtime rivals (DC) also got in on the act in 1997. In Issue 2 of *The Creeper*, the titular character's alter-ego, reporter Jack Rider, refers to his editor's managerial style: "Just a little tense in there—and not just on account of Christine's "Ghenghis (sic) Khan School of Upper Management." Ironically, Len Kaminski, the writer for that issue was not far off, because in the 21st century a simple Google Search reveals a number of articles on lessons learned from "Genghis Khan" that can be applied for business, as well as a few books, including *Managing a Dental Practice the Genghis Khan Way*.

Yet, the negative imagery of the Mongols is not restricted to the comic book world. The Mongols still served as an excellent model for "the other," particularly when one needed an intimidating and martial appearance. In Gene Roddenberry's *Star Trek* television series, the Klingons were (perhaps unintentionally) space Mongols. Appearing for the first time in episode 26 of season 1 (1967), the Klingons were swarthy (unlike the largely Caucasian crew of the Federation starship, Enterprise), with a slight "Mongolian" look to them—spare facial hair and eyebrows gave them a more Asian appearance and adjusted for a lack of an epicanthic fold. Of course, *Star Trek* aired in 1966-1969, during the period in which the United States was engaged in Vietnam and after fighting two wars with Asian powers (Japan in World War II and the Korean War in the early 1950s). This connection is strengthened in the third season in 1969 with episode 22, "Savage Curtain," in which an alien pits two teams of champions in a deadly contest to test the concepts of good versus evil. Captain Kirk teams up with Abraham Lincoln and two other good guys versus Genghis Khan and Kahless (the Klingon who unifies the Klingon race), and two other bad guys. Still, the Klingons often appeared to be remorseless, yet noble with a sense of honor one expected of a warrior race. This image did not alter drastically over time. Although the forehead and nose of the Klingon changed beginning with the first Star Trek movie (1979)—the variation later explained in the *Star Trek: Enterprise* television programs (episodes 90 and 91 in 2005)—the Klingons remained Space Mongols. Now, however, it was even more apparent, with more leather and weapons harkening to the earlier images of leather and fur-clad barbarians sweeping across the steppes. As the Klingons became more nuanced, one could also detect parallels between Kahless and the historic Chinggis Khan, refuting their original placement on Team Evil in the original *Star Trek* series.

As referenced earlier, Spider-Man was not alone in associating Genghis Khan with a tyrannical dictator. In episode 148 (1978-1979) of the television program M*A*S*H, surgeon B. J. Honeycutt refers to his bunkmate, Hawkeye, as a regular "Genghis Khan" after Hawkeye finds the mantle of leadership heavy while serving as commanding officer of the 4077th Mobile Army Surgical Hospital during Colonel Potter's absence. Using Genghis Khan here is appropriate on two levels. The first is that M*A*S*H was set during the Korean War and very much fit in with the idea of Genghis Khan as an Oriental Despot in a Wittfogelian and Weberian sense. Secondly, as this episode aired in 1978, it remains a snapshot of the mainstream western view of Chinggis Khan. It is not surprising; one method of demonizing someone's political views was to suggest that they were "to the right of Genghis Khan," an opinion that, while in vogue at the time, is quite ahistorical.

Indeed, in popular culture, Genghis Khan has become less a historical figure than a caricature or perhaps a synonym for ruthlessness, tyranny, and barbarism. Maybe the pinnacle of this use is in Miike Snow's song "Genghis Khan," with its delightful James Bondesque video, which compares the singer's jealousy to the Mongol leader, singing:

> And I don't have the right
> To ask where you go at night
> But the waves hit my head
> To think someone's in your bed
>   I get a little bit Genghis Khan
> I don't want you to get it on
> With nobody else but me
> With nobody else but me
> I get a little bit Genghis Khan

> Don't want you to get it on
> With nobody else but me.

So whither Chinggis Khan in the popular mind? The historical Chinggis Khan is slowly returning, albeit there are still risks of overly romanticizing him due to his status in Mongolia as the Founding Father. As with all Founding Father figures—whether Chinggis Khan, George Washington, Thomas Jefferson, King Alfred the Great, Charlemagne, Mao, Huangdi, or even Genghis Khan's Klingon buddy Kahless—their achievements and acts mingle reality and myth, so that their humanity is replaced with an idealized hero. Still, careful, nuanced study and appreciation of history is the best antidote to romanticized heroes or demonized caricatures.

10. Legacy of Chinggis Khan

Unbeknownst to the Tangut leaders, Chinggis Khan died on August 18, 1227. They surrendered shortly thereafter and submitted before his tent. Chinggis Khan's sons and generals accepted the submission. Yet, it was too late. The royal family of Xi Xia was executed and destroyed.

After Chinggis Khan died, his third son Ögödei became the Qa'an—emperor—of the Mongol Empire. Chinggis Khan's title also changed posthumously (although the precise date is uncertain) to Chinggis Khaghan (a rendering of Qa'an) to reflect the new reality. It was not until 1229 that Ögödei ascended the throne. The delay, in part, was because Chinggis Khan died far from home and the Tangut needed to be destroyed. Eventually, a *quriltai* was held in the Onan-Kerülen River region, Chinggis Khan's homeland. Although he had named Ögödei as successor, according to tradition there was no reason his wishes had to be respected—it was merely a suggestion, not locked in royal tradition. Yet, with his death and the delay, it allowed for the magnitude of Chinggis Khan's achievements to be properly considered. As is well known, Chinggis Khan conquered more territory than any single person in history. It is unlikely that the Mongols knew this, but at the same time, they had ventured into lands that, for them, had been previously unknown and had visited cities they had perhaps only heard of from passing merchants. A new world had been opened and Mongols came not as visitors, but as rulers. In a single lifetime, Chinggis Khan transformed the nomads from a remote corner of the steppes into the most dominant power in the world, capable of fighting two empires at once and even wiping one of the most powerful states in the world, the Khwarazmian Empire, off the map.

Chinggis Khan's achievements defied human ability compared with other leaders. Indeed, with his elevated status, Chinggis Khan entered the spirit world as a demi-god. As such, his words and wishes were not simply the pronouncements of a mere mortal ruler. They had to be respected, and so they were. While Chinggis Khan's younger brother Temüge, who served as regent of Mongolia during Chinggis Khan's foreign adventures, may have desired the throne, it was not his to inherit. Nor was it Tolui's, his talented military-minded son, even though he served as regent immediately after Chinggis Khan's death. Ögödei became the second ruler of the Mongol Empire. In his reign from 1229 to 1241, Ögödei finished the destruction of the Jin Empire, ordered Mongol troops back into Afghanistan to restore order, sent an army to hunt down the last Khwarazmshah, Jalal al-Din, and conquer Iran as well as Armenia and Georgia. He expanded the empire from the Sea of Japan to the Carpathian Mountains, with Mongol troops being spotted even on the outskirts of Vienna. Yet, he never gained the status of Chinggis Khan. Unlike his father, Ögödei left the conquests to generals, but he proved to be a talented ruler who could see things not merely in terms of black and white, but in the multi-hued complexity of reality. In addition to establishing the true administrative foundations of the Mongol Empire, Ögödei harnessed his father's success to build an ideology that *Möngke Köke Tenggeri*, The Eternal Blue Heaven, had bequeathed the earth to Chinggis Khan and his successors.

In truth, it is because of Ögödei that the empire endured beyond the spectacular success of Chinggis Khan. Without him, it is likely that Chinggis Khan's conquests and reforms would have been remembered in a way similar to how Alexander the Great is remembered—amazing and legendary, but also ephemeral—a comet flaming across the horizon that burns out all too soon. Bolstered by Ögödei's efforts, Chinggis Khan's legacy is that of the Mongol Empire. Undoubtedly, without him, the Mongol Empire would not have occurred.

While not always in vogue, the idea of Great Men (or Women) in history still has merit as Chinggis Khan certainly fits that mold. There is no reason the Mongols of all the groups in the steppe should have emerged or even to have an empire that put others to shame, but yet it happened. Chinggis Khan surrounded himself with talented individuals who carried out his vision, while also allowing them enough independence to mold it.

The most obvious legacy of the Mongol Empire is also its most important: Mongolia and the Mongolian people. Prior to the rise of the Chinggis Khan, the Mongols were just one of a dozen groups. They first appeared in history during the Tang Dynasty by that name. A Mongolian language may have existed prior to this, but it is was not known as such. When Temüjin became Chinggis Khan, his most important act was transforming all the tribes into the *Yeke Monggol Ulus*, the great Mongol Nation or state. Everyone was to be a Mongol, not a Naiman or Merkit. These older identities did not completely vanish, but instead, they became a sub-identity among the supra-group known as the Mongols.

So what did it mean to be a Mongol? It meant adopting the Mongolian culture, which was largely the same as other groups across the steppes. Yet it also included some particular aspects, such as how to slaughter animals (stilling the heart rather than slitting the throat), a distinct haircut for men, as well as the Mongolian language. To this end, Chinggis Khan also imposed a writing system. Although he remained illiterate, he recognized the importance of writing and education, ensuring that his children became literate.

Chinggis Khan did not develop his own writing system but adopted one after defeating the Naiman. Among them lived an Uighur scribe named Tatar-Tong'a. He survived the Naiman defeat, as Tatar-Tong'a impressed Chinggis Khan with his loyalty to Tayang Khan, even in defeat. Chinggis Khan then employed him to teach the Mongols to write. The Uighur writing system was based on Syriac, which the Uighurs had adopted from Nestorian missionaries. It is likely that the Naiman learned of it through their shared religious experiences. Thus, under Tatar-Tong'a's tutelage, the Mongols adopted it but wrote the script vertically instead of right to left (as one does with Semitic scripts). This script continued to be the primary one used in the Mongol Empire and knowledge of it opened doors to the detriment of those who had never learned to write it. Chinggis Khan's grandson, Khubilai, attempted to replace it with a new script, Phagspa (named after the Buddhist lama who developed it from Tibetan), as the Uighur script offered many ambiguities when writing Mongolian. Ultimately, Phagspa was meant to be used for all languages, as they based it on phonemes and not simply letters or characters. Despite imperial backing, it never became sufficiently popular and disappeared after the collapse of the Yuan Empire (1265-1370). The imperfect vertical Uighur script survived, although it too underwent several refinements through the centuries. The Manchus who formed the Qing Empire even adopted a modified version for their own language, abandoning the complicated ideograph system that the Jin Empire used for the Jurchen language. It remained the script of the Mongols during the Qing dynasty and persevered as Mongolia gained its independence in the wake of the Qing Empire's collapse in 1911.

In 1921, Mongolia became the second communist state in the world, following the example of the Soviet Union, which had aided the Mongols in keeping the Chinese out. In the 1940s, however, Mongolia adopted a modified Cyrillic alphabet. While similar events took place in the Soviet Union's Central Asia republics, the reasons were not always academic. Part of the transition was to cut the present off with the past. Within a couple of generations, few could read the old script, thus rendering the documents of aristocracy, Buddhism, and other facets disapproved by Marxist dogma as fading memories and inaccessible to the general population. At the same time, it allowed the language to be updated. Dictionaries showing the correct spellings were developed and thus words were then spelled as they were actually pronounced rather than as they had been two centuries earlier.

After the collapse of communism in the 1990s, there was a movement to return to the script of Chinggis Khan, who quickly became the figurehead for Mongolia. Therefore, writing with vertical script was re-introduced. Yet, the vertical script proves to be ill-suited, at least for now, in the modern world filled with keyboards and computers, the internet, and mobile phones. Thus, while the program to adopt the vertical script remains, it is unlikely to replace completely Cyrillic in the near future. So Cyrillic remains in place, but the vertical script still possesses its allure and continues to be used for ceremonial functions.

As Inner Mongolia (a Qing term that meant the portion nearer to Qing territory), is now part of China, the Cyrillic script was never adopted and the vertical one never abandoned. Part of this had to do with the Sino-Soviet conflict and the retention of the vertical script was part of China's attempts to woo Mongolia into China's orbit. It failed, but the Inner or Southern Mongolians retained it and continue to use and publish it in the script. While the language has changed, the writing has not, resulting in some language differences from the predominantly Khalkha Mongols of Mongolia and the Mongols of Inner Mongolia.

From beer to descendants

Yet Chinggis Khan is remembered for more than just this writing script. As indicated earlier, he has become the founding father of Mongolia. A rock song about Chinggis Khan became the anthem of protesters against the communist regime. When the party wisely allowed communism to end peacefully in Mongolia, and as the country sought an identity, they found Chinggis Khan waiting for them. His face, as portrayed in the Yuan Empire portrait now found in the Taiwan Imperial Museum, became the symbol of the country, featured on the currency of 1000 tögrögs or greater. The airport in the capital city of Ulaanbaatar (Red Hero) was renamed Chinggis Khan International from 2005 to 2020, and one can drive down Chinggis Khan avenue and attend Chinggis Khan University, or stay at the Chinggis Khan Hotel and even bank at Chinggis Khan Bank. Chinggis Khan vodka is just waiting to burst on the international scene. For the non-vodka drinkers, there is a Chinggis

Khan beer as well. While a law was passed in Mongolia to limit the use of the Chinggis Khan name in marketing, it still graces many products. Ulaanbaatar too almost became Chinggis Khan City. However, while politicians are still Chinggis Khan-crazy, the rest of Mongolia seems to have settled down a bit. He remains respected, but no longer viewed as the sole historical figure of importance, which is a good thing as there are many Mongolian figures who deserve attention.

Another legacy of Chinggis Khan is biological. Modern Mongolia has a population of roughly 3 million people, yet genetic studies tracking Y-chromosomes suggest that .5 percent of the world's male population may be related to Chinggis Khan. To put it in real numbers, as of 2020, the Earth's population was 7.8 billion people, with approximately 3.92 billion being male. Thus, the estimate of Chinggis Khan's male descendants is about 19.6 million in 2019. Twice the population of New York City and roughly the population of the Netherlands.

Could this be true? One would hope that individuals working in the field of genetics have it right. The timing of the data is correct, but I would like to throw just a slight shadow of doubt on it. Chinggis Khan certainly had enough opportunities to procreate because he had numerous wives and concubines—he was allegedly buried with 40—and Mongolian winters are notoriously cold. And when he went on campaign, one of his women always went with him. Of course, we only discuss his sons from Börte, his primary wife, as they outranked all their step-siblings. But there were also many other sons. According to Juvaini, he had 44 sons. We don't know most of their names or the exact number for that matter, but it certainly lends itself to the possibility that a Merkit (Jochi, who may or may not have been Chinggis Khan's son) could be the ancestor of the Jochid line. Of course, as I have argued earlier, there is also a strong possibility that the rumor of Jochi's questionable birth was a smear campaign to diminish his standing and thus preclude him from vying for the ultimate throne of the Mongol Empire. Regardless, if not for Chinggis Khan, Jochi's seed would not have spread so far. It would have been largely restricted to Mongolia and perhaps Siberia, as the Merkit had connections to both areas. Furthermore, being the (legitimate or not) son of Chinggis Khan gave Jochi's heir better standing and thus access to more women with whom to procreate. Either way, this prolific procreation is due to the efforts of Chinggis Khan. Considering the number found in Mongolia, however, makes one think the offspring are more likely scions of Chinggis Khan than a Merkit father. Still, as Jochi's descendants served in several regions of the Mongol Empire, it is certainly possible for his genes to have been widespread should the Merkit rumor be true.

The descendants of Chinggis Khan became royalty that dominated much of Eurasia for centuries. These were the *altan urugh* and if one could not be a member, then one wanted to marry into it. Chinggisid princesses were always desirable as they conveyed status to their husbands, who could then use the title of *güregen* or son-in-law (of Chinggis Khan), even if it was decades later. Many used this to create their own dynasties, such as the Central Asia conqueror known as Tamerlane. Others benefited from the Chinggisid prestige as well, such as Babur, the founder of the Mughal Empire, who profited from connections to Tamerlane and Chinggis Khan. Russian nobility also sought to trace their lineage through Chinggisid princes in order to establish their credentials and standing. Whether real or not was not important, it was the perception that mattered. For all the condemning of the Mongols and the myth of the Mongol yoke, the *boyars* or nobles of the Russian empire craved for additional legitimacy. Of course, rulers in Central Asia and Mongolia could maintain the direct line longer.

The Chinggis Exchange

The more immediate impact of Chinggis Khan's legacy is also that of the Mongol Empire. It is what I call the Chinggis Exchange, or the exchange of technology, people, ideas, etc., that caused a perceptible shift in history. In other words, the world was dramatically different after Chinggis Khan and the Mongol Empire than before. The Chinggis Exchange benefitted from *Pax Mongolica*—a Latin term for "Mongol Peace." Although scholars quibble over whether there really was a *Pax Mongolica*, one cannot argue that security along trade routes did not increase during the Mongol rule. While the adage that a virgin could walk from one end of the empire to the other while carrying a vase of jewels is overstated, merchants could expect safety. Patrols ensured the routes were safe and bandits destroyed, but as any law enforcement officer knows, crime is never totally eradicated. Still, the routes were a great deal more secure, as demonstrated by missionaries, merchants, spies, and others. Of course, not all who traveled did so voluntarily. The Mongols also moved people, some as captives such as many Central Asian artisans who found themselves in Mongolia. Even Muhammad Khwarazmshah's mother became a wife of Chinggis Khan and relocated to Mongolia when the Mongol armies withdrew.

Another legacy was the concept of religious tolerance. Modern readers need to be wary when encountering this concept. Religious indifference is perhaps a better term. Chinggis Khan did not adhere to a particular religion, but if he found one useful, he patronized it, though not exclusively. Daoists found great favor under his reign thanks to the Daoist sage who grudgingly departed China to meet with Chinggis Khan in Afghanistan. Chinggis Khan rewarded him by appointing him as the highest-ranking Daoist monk in his realm while also bequeathing tax exemptions on him. Christians, Buddhists, and Muslims soon also had similar experiences. The Mongols primarily wanted clergy to pray for the ruler and not cause trouble. Smaller religions, which had less political importance, such as Zoroastrianism and Judaism, did not receive tax benefits, but the Mongols also prevented persecution by other religions.

Mongol political and military models continued to be used not only by the Mongol states that originated in the dissolution of the

Mongol Empire, but even by their successors such as the Ming Empire, Muscovy, the Mughal Empire, the Ottomans, and Safavids. Gradually, many of these models evolved or were abandoned as new methods developed or technologies were introduced, but that examples from Chinggis Khan's lifetime continued to be used is a testament to his enduring influence.

As noted earlier, Chinggis Khan has not been forgotten in popular media. His appearance as "Genghis Khan" is apparent in everything from comic books, television, and movies. John Wayne played him (*The Conqueror*-1956) as did Omar Sharif (*Genghis Khan*-1965). While we may cringe at these portrayals today, we can take comfort knowing that several more recent movies have come out, including the awarding-winning *Mongol* (2007), *Genghis Khan: To the Ends of the Earth and Sea* (2007), *By the Will of Genghis Khan* (2009) and numerous others. A search on Google pulled up 20 films in which Chinggis Khan is the focus or at supporting character. Several historical novels have also placed Chinggis Khan in the spotlight, such as Conn Iggulden's *Lords of the Bow* series. As with the movies, many of the novels do not let history get in the way of the story, yet the movies and novels still have much to offer for the Chinggis Khan enthusiast.

Besides the aforementioned Miike Snow song concerning Chinggis Khan, there are several other songs, including an instrumental by Iron Maiden, as well as a song by Ace Frehley. Of course, one must not forget the German disco group Dschingis Khan with their "Dschingis Khan" and "Rocking Son of Dscingis Khan." "Dschingis Khan" has been covered by numerous groups ranging from J-Pop to heavy metal. Not surprisingly, there are several songs about or connected to Chinggis Khan by Mongolian and Inner Mongolian groups. The most recent song (2019) "The Great Chinggis Khan" came from Mongolian heavy metal band, The Hu Band. Yet, there is also a rock opera about Chinggis Khan that combines traditional Mongolian music with the rock genre. To my knowledge, they have only performed it in Mongolia.

This is but as a sampling of the legacy of Chinggis Khan. Like the massive statue of Chinggis Khan on his horse overlooking the steppes of Mongolia at Tsonjin Boldog, his legacy looms large not only over Mongolia, but also all of history and the world.

Sources

Allsen, Thomas T. "The Rise of the Mongolian Empire and Mongolian rule in north China". Pp. 321-413. In Herbert Franke and Denis Twitchett, eds, *The Cambridge History of China*, vol. 6, *Alien Regimes and border states, 907-1368*. Cambridge: Cambridge University Press, 1994.

Atwood, Christopher P., trans. "The History of the Yuan, chapter 1", *Mongolian Studies* 39 (2017): 2-80.

Atwood, Christopher P. "Jochi and the Early Western Campaigns". Pp. 35-56. In Morris Rossabi, ed., *How Mongolia Matters: War, Law, and Society*. Leiden: Brill, 2017.

Biran, Michal. *Chinggis Khan*. London: OneWorld, 2007

Biran, Michal. *The Empire of Qara Khitai in Eurasian History*. Cambridge: Cambridge University Press, 2005.

Broadbridge, Anne F. *Women and the Making of the Mongol Empire*. Cambridge: Cambridge University Press.

Curtin, Jeremiah. *The Mongols, A History*. Boston: Little, Brown, & Co., 1908.

Chih-Ch'ang, Li. *The Travels of an Alchemist*. Tr. Arthur Waley. Westport, CT: Greenwood Press, 1976.

Cleaves, Francis W., tr. and ed. *The Secret History of the Mongols*. Cambridge, Ma: Harvard University Press, 1982.

Cleaves, Francis W. "The Historicity of the Baljuna Covenant". *Harvard Journal of Asiatic Studies* 19 (1956): 357-421.

Dunnell, Ruth W. *Chinggis Khan, World Conqueror*. Boston: Longman, 2007.

Dunnell, Ruth. "The Hsi Hsia". Pp. 154-214. In Herbert Franke and Denis Twitchett, eds, *The Cambridge History of China*, vol. 6, *Alien Regimes and border states, 907-1368*. Cambridge: Cambridge University Press, 1994.

Franke, Herbert. "The Chin Dynasty". Pp. 215-320. In Herbert Franke and Denis Twitchett, eds, *The Cambridge History of China*, vol. 6, *Alien Regimes and border states*, 907-1368. Cambridge: Cambridge University Press, 1994.

"Genghis On My Mind", *Outside Magazine*, July 1996. Online: 2 May 2004. https://www.outsideonline.com/1839791/genghis-my-mind Accessed 8 August 2019.

"Genghis Khan the GREEN: Invader killed so many people that carbon levels plummeted", *Daily Mail*. 25 January 2011. Accessed 9 August 2019. https://www.dailymail.co.uk/sciencetech/article-1350272/Genghis-Khan-killed-people-forests-grew-carbon-levels-dropped.html

Howorth, Henry H. *History of the Mongols from the 9th to the 19th Century*. London: Longman, Green, and Co., 1876, 1880, 1888.

Jackson, Peter. *The Mongols and the Islamic World From Conquest to Conversion*. New Haven: Yale University Press.

Juvaini, Ata Malik. *Genghis Khan, The History of the World-Conqueror*. Tr. J. A. Boyle. Seattle: University of Washington Press, 1997.

Juzjani, Minhaj-ud-din. *Tabikat-i-Nasiri*. Tr. H. G. Raverty. Kolkata: The Asiatic Society, 2010.

Kwanten, Luc. "The Career of Muqali: a Reassessment". *The Bulletin of Sung and Yüan Studies* 14 (1978): 31-38.

Lindner, Rudi Paul. "What was a Nomadic Tribe?" *Comparative Study of Society and History* 24, no.4 (1982), 689-711.

Martin, H. D. *The Rise of Chingis Khan and His Conquest of North China*. New York: Octagon Books, 1981.

May, Timothy. *The Mongol Empire*. Edinburgh, UK: Edinburgh University Press, 2018.

May, Timothy. "To the Left of Chinggis Khan," *World History Connected*, vol. 4/1 (October, 2006). http://worldhistoryconnected.press.uillinois.edu/4.1/may.html

May, Timothy. "Jamuqa and the Education of Chinggis Khan", *Acta Mongolica* 6 (2006): 273-286.

Morgan, David. "Iran's Mongol Experience". Pp. 57-68. Inn Morris Rossabi, ed., *How Mongolia Matters: War, Law, and Society*. Leiden: Brill, 2017.

Montesquieu. *The Spirit of Laws.* Tr. Thomas Nugent. Ontario: Batoche Books, 2001.

Morgan, David. *The Mongols*, 2nd edition. Malden, MA: Blackwell, 2007.

Onon, Urgunge, trans. *The Secret History of the Mongols: The Life and Times of Chinggis Khan* New York: RoutledgeCurzon, 2001.

Pow, Stephen. "The Last Campaign and Death of Jebe Noyan". *Journal of the Royal Asiatic Society* 27, no. 1 (2017): 31-51.

Rachewiltz, Igor de, tr. and ed. *The Secret History of the Mongols: a Mongolian epic chronicle of the thirteenth century.* Leiden: Brill, 2004.

Rachewitltz, Igor de, tr. *The Secret History of the Mongols: a Mongolian epic chronicle of the thirteenth century.* Ed. John C. Street. Canberra: Igor de Rachewiltz, 2015. https://cedar.wwu.edu/cedarbooks/4/

Rashuddin Fazlullah, *Jami'u't-Tawarikh: Compendium of Chronicles*, tr. Wheeler M. Thackston London: I. B. Tauris, 2012.

Ratchnevsky, Paul. *Genghis Khan: His Life and Legacy.* Trans. Thomas Nivison Haining. Cambridge, MA: Blackwell, 1992.

Sneath, David. *The Headless State: Aristocratic Orders, Kinship Society and Misrepresentations of Nomadic Inner Asia.* New York: Columbia University Press, 2007.

Togan, Isenbike. *Flexibility and Limitation in Steppe Formations: The Kerait Khanate and Chinggis Khan.* Leiden: Brill, 1998.

Twitchett, Denis and Klaus-Peter Tietze. "The Liao". Pp. 45-153. In Herbert Franke and Denis Twitchett, eds, *The Cambridge History of China*, vol. 6, *Alien Regimes and border states, 907-1368.* Cambridge: Cambridge University Press, 1994.

Waldron, Arthur. *The Great Wall of China: From History to Myth.* Cambridge: Cambridge University Press, 1990.

Wang, Jinping. *In the Wake of the Mongols: The Making of a New Social Order in North China, 1200-1600.* Cambridge, MA: Harvard University Asia Center, 2018.

Weatherford, Jack. *Genghis Khan and the Making of the Modern World.* New York: Crown, 2004.

Weatherford, Jack, *Genghis Khan and the Quest for God: How the World's Greatest Conqueror Gave Us Religious Freedom* (New York: Viking, 2016).

Wittfogel, Karl. *Oriental Despotism: A Comparative Study of Total Power*. New Haven: Yale University Press, 1957.

Zhao Hong. *Meng Da Bei Lu*. Trans. N. Ts. Munkueva. Moscow: NAUKA, 1975.

Suggested Reading

Citations have been kept to a minimum, but as with all historical studies, my research rests on sources from the period and other scholars. As the primary audience for this book is not the academic world, I have restricted the citations and suggested readings to those in English. The study of Chinggis Khan and the Mongol Empire, however, requires a plethora of languages ranging in no particular order from Mongolian, Chinese, Persian, Russian, Japanese, Korean, Latin, Armenian, Georgian, Arabic, Church Slavonic, French, Old French, and many more. Rarely will one find a scholar who can use more than a handful of the original languages, making the study of the Mongol Empire a truly collaborative effort. You can find the full bibliographic detail in the sources section.

The key source to the study of Chinggis Khan's life is *The Secret History of the Mongols* (SHM). It is our only detailed source in Mongolian and has been translated several times. For this book, I use Igor de Rachewiltz's translation (Leiden: Brill, 2004). Rather than page numbers, I cite by section (§), so that the reader may find the reference regardless of edition or translation. The suggested reading also includes Urgunge Onon and Francis Cleaves' translations as well as references to the abridged ebook version of Rachewiltz's translation. The abridgment does not affect the text, only the notes. The actual author of *The Secret History of the Mongols* is unknown, although some have long suspected that it was initially written by Shiqi Qutuqu, although other possibilities exist. The text was long lost, but a version survived as a Ming textbook for translators. It has been reconstructed into Mongolian, although sections of it have also been found in later Mongolian texts such as the *Altan Tobchi* or Golden Chronicle, which have greatly aided in the reconstruction.

Another important source is *Jami'at al-Tawarikh* (JT), a Persian chronicle written by the polymath Rashid al-Din, who served as the vizier of Ghazan Khan, a great-great-grandson of Chinggis Khan. Rashid al-Din's work was written in the late 13th and 14th centuries. It offers a different perspective and does not always agree with *The Secret History*. It does, however, draw upon material (in many cases copied) from the *Shengwu qinzheng lu*, also known as the *Campaigns of the Holy Warrior*. This Chinese text was written in a Mongolian idiom, suggesting that there was originally a Mongolian version and the Chinese is a copy. Unfortunately, the Mongolian is lost. An English translation is in process, but not yet published, although a dated French edition known as the *Histoire des campagnes de Genghis Khan* was made by the eminent scholar Paul Pelliot in 1951.

While not as useful as information about the rise of Chinggis Khan, the Persian history *Tarikh-i Jahan Gusha* by Ata Malik Juvaini is crucial for understanding the campaign against the Khwarazmian Empire. Translated by J. A. Boyle and published in English as *The History of the World-Conqueror*, it covers much more than the title implies. While Juvaini's father witnessed the Mongol invasion of the Khwarazmian Empire and then found employment with the Mongols, Juvaini was in the court of Hülegü, Chinggis Khan's grandson, who led the conquest of much of the Middle East in the 1250s. He leaves us with an insightful but biased history about the life of Chinggis Khan until 1256, omitting Hülegü's sack of Baghdad, where Juvaini later served as governor. Boyle's translation perfectly captures Juvaini's purple prose and retains the highly stylized nature of the original text. The final Persian historian references come from Juzjani, who fled from the Khwarazmian Empire to the safety of Delhi in India. From the Delhi Sultanate, Juzjani wrote his *Tabikat-i Nasiri*, which was a history of the various Muslim dynasties that had appeared since the days of the Prophet Muhammad. Juzjani ended his work with the considerable section on the "Irruption of the Mongols" which extends into 1260. Juzjani was clearly biased against the Mongols and thus one can expect a negative slant to most of his comments, yet he also serves as a nice counterbalance to the accounts of Rashid al-Din and Juvaini.

Besides the *Shengwu qinzheng lu*, the prominent Chinese source for the life of Chinggis Khan is the official history of the Mongol Empire, known as the *Yuan shi* (YS). It follows the style and structure of all official Chinese dynastic histories, including being organized by the dynasty that followed the subject. Thus, the *Yuan shi* (Yuan being the dynastic name taken by Chinggis Khan's grandson, Khubilai Khan) was compiled during the Ming Dynasty (1368-1644). As many of the officials involved in the project included members of the former Yuan bureaucracy, one can argue that the Yuan government was also involved, such as the leading figure in the project, Song Lian. Chapter 1 is devoted to the life of Chinggis Khan and has been recently translated and published in English by Christopher P. Atwood of the University of Pennsylvania.

For the benefit of the reader, I have generally eschewed referring to primary sources in their original language or a non-English translation, but I would be remiss if I did not mention Zhao Hong's *Meng Da Bei Lu*. This account from a Song envoy to Chinggis Khan is the only source that states that Chinggis Khan was in the Jin Empire in his youth. It also has a detailed account of the Mongols, their lives, and culture. The final Chinese source consulted was *The Travels of an Alchemist*, as titled by the translator Arthur Waley. It was written by Li Chih-Ch'ang, an acolyte of the Daoist sage, Changchun. This account traces the journey of Changchun from China to Mongolia and then to his meeting and time he spent with Chinggis Khan in Central Asia.

I would also refer the reader to three important biographies of Chinggis Khan, which provide slightly different perspectives and excellent erudition, should the reader wish to continue their study of Chinggis Khan. The first, arranged alphabetically by author, is Michal Biran's (Hebrew University, Jerusalem) *Chinggis Khan* (2007). Biran, one of the leading scholars of the Mongol Empire, has produced a unique study of Chinggis Khan, which not only serves as a commendable biography, but also attempts to understand

Chinggis Khan's impact on the Islamic world. As part of the late Patricia Crone's *Makers of the Muslim World* series, Chinggis Khan may seem an odd addition, but Biran's work highlights how the Islamic world changed because of Chinggis Khan. Biran's work also examines the Mongol leader's legacy across Eurasia. Ruth W. Dunnell's (Kenyon College) *Chinggis Khan, World Conqueror* (2010) is the second recommended biography. It was written with undergraduate students in mind. Concise and with several charts, maps, and glossaries, it remains ideal for classroom use and an introduction to Chinggis Khan's life. As a specialist on Xi Xia and medieval Chinese history, Dunnell's perspective and focus differs from Biran, but is equally useful.

The third of the recommend biographies is Paul Ratchnevsky's classic, *Genghis Khan: His Life and Legacy*, originally published in Germany as *Činggis-Khan: Sein Leben und Wirken* in 1983. Thomas Nivison Haining adeptly translated it and moved some of the context from the footnotes directly into the text to create an accessible and very learned biography. Produced during the Cold War, it retains some of the Marxist approach. Interpretation aside, Ratchnevsky's work remains the best academic biography on Chinggis Khan and helps clarify some aspects of Chinggis Khan's life.

In 2004, Jack Weatherford of Macalester College published *Genghis Khan and the Making of the Modern World*, which became a New York Times bestseller. Beautifully written, it captures the imagination and did much to elevate Chinggis Khan out of the shadow of Genghis Khan in popular opinion. While recounting the life of Chinggis Khan, Weatherford also examined the long-term impact of the Mongols. Although Weatherford's enthusiasm is contagious, it also sometimes exaggerated the impact of the Mongols and downplayed their ruthlessness as well. Yet, despite its historical inaccuracies, his anthropological insights offer a different and worthwhile perspective, and his engaging writing style also makes it an ideal "gateway" to the study of the Mongol Empire for the uninitiated. Weatherford's *Genghis Khan and the Quest for God: How the World's Greatest Conqueror Gave Us Religious Freedom* also merits reading. In this, his third book, Weatherford examines Chinggis Khan's interest in religion and argues that the policies established in the Mongol Empire would later influence Thomas Jefferson and others in their understanding of separation of church and state, and religious tolerance in the United States. While seemingly far-fetched, Weatherford makes an appealing case while tracing the influences from the 13th to the 18th century. Yet, as with all of his works, Weatherford's exuberance sometimes strays away from the facts and into speculation. Still, it is quite thought-provoking.

Anne F. Broadbridge, *Women and the Making of the Mongol Empire* is, in some sense, a "revisionist history." Broadbridge (University of Massachusetts-Amherst) expands our understanding of Mongolian history and society by putting the role of Mongolian women in the spotlight. Her study of the role of the queens and daughters of Chinggis Khan reveals the complexity of Chinggis Khan's alliances and administrative system. While it has long been understood that wives served as advisors and councilors, Broadbridge's groundbreaking work shows how their roles and relations extended far beyond the role of counselor.

As mentioned in the text, the subject of tribes and their organization is one that generates much debate among historians and anthropologists. My points of discussion stem primarily from two works. My definition of "tribe" originates with Rudi Linder's (University of Michigan) classic article, "What was a Nomadic Tribe." Although his discussion focused on the Huns, his salient points can be applied to other Central Eurasian steppes nomads as well. David Sneath's (Cambridge University) *The Headless State* is also very useful and thought-provoking, although controversial in some circles. He argues forcefully that we should look at tribal confederation states as states and not be tied to the Eurocentric Westphalian interpretation that has dominated the discourse on states and politics for so long.

While academic articles can be difficult for the non-specialist, I refer to a few works throughout this book. The relationship between

Jamuqa and Temüjin continues to intrigue scholars, but Jamuqa's status as a military leader and Temüjin's military training have received attention in only one study, titled "Jamuqa and the Education of Chinggis Khan" by this author. The individuals who drank the muddy waters of Lake Baljuna are explored in Francis W. Cleaves' "The Historicity of the Baljuan Covenant." While at Harvard, Cleaves was the dominant American scholar in the study of the early Mongol Empire. Stephen Pow's "The Last Campaign and Death of Jebe Noyan", briefly examines the life of the Mongol general Jebe, before focusing on his and Sübedei's epic *reconnaissance en force*. Pow argues that Jebe is the mysterious Mongol vanguard commander who died at the Battle of Kalka River in 1223. In his "Iran's Mongol Experience," David Morgan, a specialist on the Mongols in Iran, explored the Mongols reputation for destruction and found that, while they were indeed brutal, it may not have been quite as bleak as one may have thought. In the same volume, one will also find Christopher P. Atwood's article assessing Jochi's military career, which then leads to questions about his depiction in the sources. Luc Kwanten's article on the career of Muqali is a nice exploration of this general's career but also sheds light on the events leading to the ultimate destruction of Xi Xia.

There are many works that provide an appropriate overview of the Mongols' neighbors; those that follow are but a sampling. The best overview of Xi Xia remains Ruth Dunnell's "The Hsi Hsia." The old Wade-Giles system of transliterating Chinese spelled Xi Xia is found in the sixth volume of the mammoth *Cambridge History of China* series. As the sixth volume, *Alien Regimes and Border States*, 907-1368, focuses on "Alien Regimes" or dynasties ruled by non-Han Chinese, readers will find chapters on the Liao Dynasty by Denis Twitchett and Klaus-Peter Tietze, and Jin Dynasty by Herbert Franke and several excellent chapters on the Mongol Empire as well. For these, the most pertinent for this work is Thomas T. Allsen's "The rise of the Mongolian empire and Mongolian rule in north China." I should note that this work was published when the system of transliterating Chinese characters into Latin letters changed, thus some names will be drastically different/for instance, instead of Jin, we see Chin. The pronunciation remains the same, though. Michal Biran's masterful work, *The Empire of Qara Khitai in Eurasian History*, will undoubtedly serve as the standard work for Qara Khitai for decades to come. Detailed studies of the other tribes that existed alongside the Mongols are rare, but one on the Kereit exists. In *Flexibility and Limitation in Steppe Formations: The Kereit Khanate and Chinggis Khan*, the Turkish scholar Isenbike Togan (Middle East Technical University, Ankara) focuses on the rise of the Kereit Khanate of Toghril Ong-Khan and the Mongols' place in that history. Her study of the dynamics among Yisügei, Chinggis Khan, and the Kereit fleshes out the detailed but often vague descriptions provided in *The Secret History of the Mongols* and other sources. Jinping Wang's *In the Wake of the Mongols* examines the aftermath of the Mongol Conquest in the Jin Empire. In it, she explores how local Chinese communities changed and how new powerful institutions, such as Quanzhen Daoism and Buddhism, shaped Chinese society while Confucianism declined in importance.

While not about Chinggis Khan, for a proper understanding of the Great Wall of China, and the use of defensive walls in history, as well as the mythology that arose around the Great Wall, Arthur Waldron's classic *The Great Wall of China: From History to Myth*, remains required reading. Besides the primary sources, H. D. Martin's classic work, *The Rise of Chingis Khan and His Conquest of North China*, is a useful study as well, not only on the campaigns in Xi Xia and the Jin Empire, but also the Mongol military. On the latter aspect, it is dated, having been originally published in 1950. Thus, the chapter on "The Art of War" is derived from this author's *The Mongol Art of War* published in 2007, and then corrected in a paperback edition in 2016.

Several books provide the general history of the Mongol Empire., including this author's *The Mongol Empire* (Edinburgh: Edinburgh University Press, 2018). Written as part of The Edinburgh History of Islamic Empires, May's work provides a narrative history of the Mongol Empire from its origins until the last edifices of the empire disappear and form new states, while also analyzing the Mongols' relationship with Islam and the gradual conversion to Islam by three-quarters of the Empire. This work is also one of the few that seeks to understand the empire primarily from the perspective of the conquerors rather than the conquered. Another book that examines the Mongols relationship with Islam is Peter Jackson's masterful *The Mongols and the Islamic World From Conquest to Conversion*. Jackson's work, as the title suggests, focuses on the Islamic World and will be a source from which scholars benefit for decades to come.

For well over 20 years, the standard book on the Mongols was appropriately titled *The Mongols* and written by David Morgan. He published it in 1986 while he taught at the University of London. After undergoing over 20 reprints and being translated into many languages, the publishers finally convinced Professor Morgan to publish a second edition in 2007 while he was at the University of Wisconsin. Rather than revise the entire manuscript, Morgan added a new chapter, which reviewed the new scholarship on the Mongols since 1990 (when a corrected paperback edition came out). Thus, while much of the book often reflects some now-outmoded ideas of the Mongols, it remains valuable because it brilliantly shows the development of the study of the Mongols over the past three decades and should be on the reading list of any serious student of the Mongol Empire.

Two older studies have also been referenced. Henry H. Howorth's multi-volume *History of the Mongols from the 9th to the 19th Century* is the first, while the second is Jeremiah Curtin's, *The Mongols, A History*. With Howorth's written in the 19th century and Curtin's in the early 20th century, both are out of date, but readers curious to see the changing views of the Mongol Empire through time may find them useful. Scholars can still benefit from perusing them, as they often contain forgotten nuggets of information that found interest in the author's time period but have become less fashionable today. More importantly, it remains useful to understanding how the field has developed and who laid the foundation for the study of the Mongols.

Many more works exist, but those mentioned above should whet the appetite of any reader interested in Chinggis Khan and the Mongols.

About the Author

Timothy May is Professor of Central Eurasian History at the University of North Georgia. He is the author of *The Mongols* (2019), *The Mongol Empire* (2018), *The Mongol Conquests in World History* (2012), and *The Mongol Art of War* (2007), among many other publications, and serves as the editor of the journal *Mongolian Studies*. May is a frequent presenter at national and international conferences and has won many awards for his educational activities.

A Word from the Publisher

Thank you for reading *Simply Chinggis*!

If you enjoyed reading it, we would be grateful if you could help others discover and enjoy it too.

Please review it with your favorite book provider such as Amazon, BN, Kobo, Apple Books, or Goodreads, among others.

Again, thank you for your support and we look forward to offering you more great reads.

www.ingramcontent.com/pod-product-compliance
Lightning Source LLC
Chambersburg PA
CBHW030152100526
44592CB00009B/243